Hi! This is Katy

Wallace Tooke

Swanton, Ohio

Book Design and Layout by Elizabeth "B.J." Lord
Cover Illustration by Sue Revenaugh

Printed in the United States of America

ISBN 0-9646835-0-4

This book is dedicated to

Katy,
my wife Josephine,
and one of our closest
and most supportive
friends,
Dr. C. Lance West, D.C., D.I.B.A.K.

My thanks to the following people:

Marilyn Schafstall for typing, re-typing,
and proofing the galleys, as well as her
continued support from the
beginning of this project;

to Nancy Rossnagel for encouraging
me to seek publication and putting me in touch
with someone who could do that,
and also for her continued support
through production and distribution;

grateful thanks to Sue Revenaugh
for taking on the dauntless task of creating
a cover illustration that represents
so well the action of this book;

thanks to B.J. Lord for taking on the job of getting
this book published, her time and effort in
researching methods and all the little details that
go into such a project, and for sticking with
it until completion; and

heartfelt thanks to my son, Walter,
for committing himself to
the completion of this book,
no matter what.

Introduction

"Miracle of the Ages" is a wide spread topic these days. It serves as a survival kit for the far reaching mania that is spreading like a creeping paralysis over the minds of people the world over. The age in which we live is very materialistic and the theme of today is *getting into one's self.* This opens up a torrent of inner human passions and emotions that have long been buried. In our self-discovery, humans are resurrecting long buried desires, not knowing just how to adequately deal with their deep seated feelings.

Although we are bringing these feelings to the surface for correction, the deeper we probe into the human element, the more we are opening Pandora's Box. The context of this dilemma is not a matter of moralizing nor self criticism, but a matter much in need of explanation and solution.

The contents of this book of transcriptions came as a shock and surprise to me. Originally, it was not my intention to reveal these truths publicly or openly. However, after eight years of receiving these messages, I became aware that there are many human beings searching for answers to mysteries of the beyond. While in the beginning I believed these to be personal messages, as time went on it became apparent to me that they were intended to be for those who are seriously interested in the search for continued life. Herein is the reason for opening these discourses to others.

The information in this book is a search for rightful solutions and a probing for answers. The question has always been asked, "What is the solution for human suffering?" In exercising our ability to seek answers and to discover a way out of this dilemma, we have done extensive research and yet seem to be no closer to the answer than we were before.

My background is similar to most American families. As a child I lived in Kansas City, Missouri. My mother was a Methodist and my father came from an Episcopalian teaching. I first attended St. James Catholic School, but by the time I entered third grade my mother thought it best to transfer me from parochial school to public school, which I attended for the rest of my school years. My early religious training included going to Sunday School and singing in the Memorial Boys Choir of an Episcopal Church. At this young age I was fascinated by the ritual, but when it came time to listen to the sermons I was unable to capture the message or true meaning. Back in my mind, however, there has always been a gnawing desire to know more about the soul and the Kingdom of God.

My mother's mother had very little education, but was extremely psychic. She never attended any spiritual churches or meetings but held steadfastly to her own beliefs.

On maturity I went on to become a minister, having attended the Unity School of Christianity in Lee's Summit, Missouri. I later married Josie, a Catholic girl, to whom I am still happily united. This information is relayed to you so that you may understand that I have a fairly open mind and am not prejudiced by any former established concepts or beliefs.

Long before this story begins, I went through a lengthy struggle and search for what I choose to term reality. As a child, I was mystified by the departure of souls in death — those whom I now consider transcending to another dimension. At an early age I knew nothing of transition other than the ordinary term death. From my religious background, I followed the traditional explanation of the soul going to either heaven or hell. This never entirely met with my own concepts, although I had no idea at the time just what transaction really took place. As a child, I would often look up into the sky and wonder to which star my loved ones had journeyed. I could never visualize them in either heaven or hell as I was taught to do by church theology. As far back as I can remember, I was always interested in the soul. I read every book I could find about the soul but never did any enlightenment come. I went to the public library in search of knowledge about the soul only to discover that they could not satisfy my quest.

After I had been a minister for several years I visited a woman patient who was in the hospital for senility and many physical problems. I meditated with the lady and was about to leave when she said, "Before you go, will you pray for me?" Obligingly I sat back down, realizing that I should pray for her soul and that would include every part of her. From an inner voice I heard the words, "Man does not have a soul." At first I was startled, and my first impression was that this must be devil talk — only I was very calm and peaceful. I inwardly thought, "This must be coming from God." Again the words came, "Man does not have a soul." With the third time I heard these words, I quietly inquired, "God, please reveal to me the meaning of this." It was then that a strong authoritative voice spoke. "Man does not *have* a soul . . . man *is* a soul." With great relief and composure I answered the woman's request for prayer. But the memory of those words, "Man does not *have* a soul . . . man *is* a soul" opened the way for me to understand the subject of the soul.

It wasn't until much later in life, after my attempt to read everything I could on the subject, that I was given a set of Britannica's "Great Books of the Western World". Through these books I became quite familiar with the many great philosophers of the world. The most fascinating of all the 54 volumes were about Plato and Plotinus. Here I spent many hours in learning more than I ever believed possible about the soul from the Greek philosophers of centuries ago. I say, "I ever believed possible", yet inwardly a chord was struck as though this was what I had been looking for all my life and, in some strange way, seemed most familiar.

This world is under the influence of material powers. The present generation has made great scientific discoveries about the world and outer space through the space program and the discovery of atomic energy. The new computer age has hastened our researching with incredible speed and accuracy. For the most part, all societies are getting more into materialistic, so-called realism, and yet are having a difficult time in adjusting to the change and the challenge it presents.

We are certainly satisfied with the modern convenience of our living conditions, not to mention the acceleration in medical discoveries which have lengthened life on this planet. It certainly is a great age in which to be alive and remain so for as long as possible.

Religion has lost most of its flare because conditions here are much more exciting, pleasing and satisfying than at any other time in history. The deplorable conditions in which humans lived in ages past, including slavery, intrigue, deprivation, and crude living conditions, forced them to seek some solace in a better life to come in some distant heaven or happy hunting ground. Such is not the case today. Heaven has lost the visionary pleasure from dreary human strife. It appears that more interesting experiences are going on right here on good old terra firma.

Nevertheless, recent fears have sprung up about radiation, polluted air and streams, together with more deadly diseases that may erase our temporal life. Once again we have been accosted with fear and dread, only in a different disguise and form. Many feel that with each nation pointing a giant bomb at another nation, there is little hope for this civilization. Having lost interest in the dull outlook for attaining heaven, civilization seems to have nowhere to turn. Survival is the cry of today. It has always been and will continue to be. The question we might ask is: *Survival of what?* If I am to survive, what is there that will continue in this eternal stream of life that is worth attaining?

The following is a true story which I experienced a few years ago. It has been kept confidential except for my wife, Josie, and a close friend. At first I was reluctant to reveal this material. It wasn't until recently that I had the approval and permission to disclose what I am about to relate.

Approximately 30 years ago, a young woman started attending some of the metaphysical classes I was teaching. As the months rolled past, my wife and I became close friends with this woman and her husband as we searched together for the truth about life. Time passed and suddenly, over some misunderstanding about affairs of our church organization, our friendship ceased abruptly. My Capricornian nature left me puzzled and hurt. For several years little or no communication existed between us until there was a reconciliation.

My wife had become much closer to this woman than I. The woman was a musician and an artist, although I only became aware of her skill as an artist after her death. The latter few years were much more pleasant, although not what you would call chummy, until a severe illness of long duration became evident. The remaining year of which I speak brought about a sudden contact which became more complete than ever before. The time was drawing near for her departure. Not until this woman expired did the whole drama begin.

The afternoon following her funeral, which I myself conducted, I went home depressed. I experienced the usual bereavement of a friend, and I discovered it to be a closer friendship than I had ever dreamed. Feeling a bit unsettled, I decided to do something to shake off my unexplainable grief and concern. My feelings were not of fear or about going to heaven or hell as they might have been in the past. I decided to go out in the beautiful afternoon and do something physical, like cutting the grass, which I was obliged to do anyway.

While I was about my business of cutting the grass I continued to feel sad, especially when the realization came to me that this woman was no more. I had this sudden, climactic sound in my mind. Not a sensation of hearing, but as I thought it to be then, in my mind. I actually heard this lady say, in her voice but in my mind —"dikes, dams and ditches". I was overwhelmed. I questioned why she would be talking about a subject which we had never discussed or mentioned before. I immediately went into the house and told my wife. She, too, was surprised and amazed. At this point I didn't know what was happening or just what I was experiencing. What was I to do about this strange behavior? Who could I speak to about it?

I decided to go to her husband and ask. But how was I to approach such a thing to a person who might think I was crazy or obsessed? Still the urge was too strong and the puzzle too deep for me to restrain myself. I thought for a moment and decided to state the situation in a way that might not be too direct and side-track the issue. I made the visit and was greeted by her husband, who was at this early time in stress over his loss. Still motivated by my decision to inquire, I went ahead, spoke consoling words and then asked, "Did your wife ever discuss such matters as 'dikes, dams, and ditches' with you?"

He said, "Why yes. Just a few days ago she was discussing such matters. Being on the board of a local park commission she was telling me about the suggested changes at the Park."

I was very relieved but did not disclose to him what I had heard. This in no way explained what had happened, although I felt a closeness with this woman such as I had never felt before. Several days later I began to feel more of a presence from her, and then I heard the announcement, "Hi! This is Katy."

Yes, that was her name — Katy.* This is when the plot began to thicken and the rest of this book are communications that came over the next few years. In the beginning the communications were brief, but as time progressed they became more provocative.

That first message, "Hi! This is Katy", was just the beginning!

---

*Ed. Note: We have changed the name to protect the privacy of members of her family who still remain. Other than the author and his wife, all other names of living persons have been changed.

June 30, 1983

Oh, I'm so excited! Today I had quite a revelation. I saw a fly. Don't act startled. Yes, it was a fly. Seemed so strange to see a fly here. First one I saw. It was the same but different. It was transparent and translucent. From what I gather, it is the existing prototype of the flies you have on your planet. Seems so strange to say "on your planet", but I'm here now. Lots of things to discover. Never know what I'm going to discover next.

From what I have gathered so far — everything you have on your planet has its beginning here. Here is the workshop or factory — that's the only way I can explain it — of everything you have now or you are going to have.

Seems everyone here is working out progressive ideas that you will begin to discover and use on your plane. Not too clear about it all yet, but just giving you some ideas as to how it is here.

I saw your mother yesterday — she sure is cute. She is having a harder time understanding all that is, and all that is going on, on this side, but she is jovial and seems very happy.

The reason she seemed sad to you yesterday is because she is unable to reach you. She said it's like you were so far away. She looked at me and smiled. Don't worry about her. She is O.K.

Bit by bit I am learning about this place. There is so much to grasp and learn. It is not that difficult, only it does take a while to get used to.

Colors and dyes interest me. They are really something to see. Like the fly, which is beautiful and has an earthly purpose. People shouldn't kill them like they do even though they are a nuisance. They have a very important part to play. Everything on earth does — so I'm learning.

July 6, 1983

Try writing slower. You think I am speaking too fast. I am not sending you a message as those on your planet would send a message. What you are receiving is not from my mind, because, as you are aware, I have no brain. This is coming by way of my subconscious mind. Something of me is conscious of this communication, but, as yet, I am not knowledgeable in explaining it to you.

You did get my message last night before you went to bed. I am aware of your depression and only remind you of a way out. You received the message: "It's a great world, a wonderful world, a great and wonderful world." I could sense the intenseness with which you received it. Josie will know what I mean, because I am aware how she likes to use the *Daily Word* for an inspirational start. Listen to her more. It works, and you have been disillusioned as to its usage. Think about this, and tell Josie she is right again.

Josie, you should be able to pick up on me, too. This communication pleases me, for no one else is able to hear my inner voice. Not yet, anyway, or perhaps this is the way it is intended to be for now. I have no prophetic abilities now. Perhaps in future development I will be able to explain more.

You would not know or recognize me as I am now. I do not even feel I have lost my human form. There was the momentary period of my transition when I was, to human sense, afraid, and when I had some physical discomfort, but this is all as nothing now. I feel very much the same as I did on earth only much happier and truly free. We can all identify and recognize each other here with no difficulty. The human instrument, the physical body, which uses five senses, cannot understand nor acknowledge this. There is absolutely nothing to fear. We are all very much the same but having no sense faculties we have no difficulty. We are aware of other forces which enable us to continue, much in the same way as we did on your plane, without the pain and agonies with which earth is infected. At least, that is the way human nature interprets it — but not as it really is.

You were right in assuming I was angry when you deleted the *Lord's Prayer* from the Sunday service. I felt comfortable saying and hearing it. True, I was bitter as you thought. I had a lot of fear at that time and was truly out of character. I had the idea that saying the prayer would make everything right, would make right things happen.

At least I was partly right, but didn't understand until I arrived here. I started this message to you this morning, and you stopped me until you had time to write it down.

You see, where I was right, and wrong, in hurting you — was in my dilemma in comprehension: "Thy will be done on earth as it is in heaven". Now I understand

— as I said before — everything begins on this plane, as existing ideas are given to us for explanation and a sort of blueprint that needs to be worked out in the ideal.

You receive these ideas third hand, so to speak. The secondary, or primitive ideas, seem to come to us from some higher force and are for us to work out in more detail. After we have finished with the working hypothesis for your safe and accurate delivery — we give you the plan. It was not clear to me about ". . . on earth as it is in heaven." I believed this (where I am now) was heaven but quickly learned I was wrong. There seems to be in me a knowing of the true pattern, but I was upset when I thought you were wrecking the plan.

You, and especially Josie, brought this to my attention in a much clearer way, but it was not until I got here that I discovered the real truth. All is well now, as you say. I know your difficulties in understanding all this, as this was my problem in understanding what you were saying. Yes, I was angry, and I am sorry for how I acted.

You and Josie have a real good truth. Keep up the fine work, and I will do all in my power to do whatever I can.

July 12, 1983

Wallace, I cannot seem to reach you and Josie at this time, as I seem to be going through some post transitional period. Be patient with me until I can determine just what it is within me that prevents the passage. I am somewhat disturbed at the blank in my transcriptions, but I am certain that it will soon pass.

There is a guide who seems to be informing me of certain transgressions on my part. Help me to understand this mystery. I must have done or said something to complicate this blockage. Help me, please.

July 13, 1983

Hi! This is Katy,

I have been waiting to contact you and Josie. The help came quickly. Some of my old fears returned, but I am all right now. You know, I can't quite get over this place. It is more wonderful than I ever imagined. All the time I feared taking this step, and now that I am here, words fail me in stating the tranquility and peace. You should be able to hear my voice distinctly and recognize it as me.

In translating to you I am to give my name, the name you know. It is for your protection, and, by so doing, you should distinguish me more vividly.

Why, I can't believe how much different this is from what I expected! No wonder people on earth have such a hard time trying to understand what it is like here. No words can describe it. I know I never had the capacity or ability to comprehend fully what it is like here, or ever could dream what it would be like.

Josie, you and I talked more than Wallace and I. I thought I believed in the things we discussed and really wanted to, but I had such a protective mind. Now it all seems so clear. Guess I absorbed more than I thought I did. I don't know of any way to relate to you conditions here. You two have a better realization and awareness than I ever did. I pictured life after life from my opinionated view. I cannot say it is true of you or others, but it was difficult for me to get out of the old framework of thinking and viewing. It was like a great diffusion or abstraction that did not enable me to ascend to a higher level of knowing. Just like I did not have the capacity or ability to break through to see the entire picture. Perhaps it is like that for all earthlings.

My energy is running out for now. More later.

August 3, 1983 / 11:45 p.m.

Remote though it may be, this is the way it is supposed to be. You are inclined to believe that there are
three weeks in a year in which you are to honor the
heavenly, celestial existence of a God. But you are wrong.
There is no such . . . *(jumbled)*.

There are twenty-four hour days in your solar system, but such is not the case in the circulatory laws of a
higher configuration. You must be alert to the on-going
movement of time, and allow it to brief you as to the
breech in your time element. Be on your guard as to the
system of time to which you are accustomed. The customary way in which you perceive or calculate time is incorrect. Measure it by time impulses . . . *(blur)*.

Exact timing is a matter of sequential difference.

August 4, 1983 / 11:30 p.m.

Hi! This is Katy,

The message you received last night, earth index time, did not come from me. If you remember, you did not receive my specific energy field. I am not this advanced as yet to give to you the data you received. What you received was from my instructor and guide. He was aware of my ability to reach you and tried, as an experiment, to see your receptivity. *(Pause)*

If you will carefully survey the instructions you received, you will be properly instructed as to their interpretation.

I am not prepared to monitor what was sent to you, but believe me — whatever it was — give it your closest attention.

August 6, 1983 / 4:30 p.m.

Hi! This is Katy,

There is a need to exercise or vent the parlance necessary to bring forth closer communication of minds. When I speak of mind, I am not referring to the use of a human faculty with which you are familiar and accustomed. We here on this plane have a different device, as you would call it, or instrument, through which to communicate our feelings and experiences.

You are wondering what kind of a body we are wearing. The body with which we are exemplifying ourselves is not something adjunct to us, but it is in a sense the closest embodiment of the true spirit which we are. Thus, you could say, we have no body, but we are visible and identifiable to each other. We can communicate, we can travel, we can experience things just as you do.

You see, Wallace, the light rays through which we focus are not identifiable with your perceptive vision. This does not mean we are unable to move about, play, work or do our bidding.

As for food consumption — as you know, dietary

demands are also different. We do not consume edible foods as you do, because we have no palate or digestive organs to contend with. Neither are we handicapped by visual or oral sounds. Our bodies act much like a light bearing substance — something like a secretion of amber waves.

(Pause)

Yes, this is Katy, but in an altered state of thought from which you knew me, even the other times I communicated with you.

I can also detect you are having a difficult time in wandering off in your own thought forms when you transcribe these messages. Do not think or try to form any images or phrase any . . .

August 11, 1983 / 3:30 p.m.

"I must give it to you in blind, by Neptunal Sea. A colorful array of pictures."

(The explanation of this transmission came later and can be found on page 195.)

August 14, 1983 / 1:40 p.m.

Hi! This is Katy,

Noble are you, Wallace. Nobler still are the deeds you perform and the lessons you deliver. Rest and let me talk to you. Let my hand guide yours. You can be certain that as I present to you these messages, I will try to be as exact as possible, as you are entitled to benefit and receive. At present, you are using your mind to interpret what I have to say. Relax more, think less, and let me guide your hand. There are volumes which I wish to communicate to you. You are still puzzled at this communication with you, but you will become accustomed to receiving the word and will profit by it.

I love you and Josie and don't really know how I would have managed as well as I did without your friendship. I was not aware of your love and consideration of me until the last few months of my existence on the earth plane. In fact, I have not only lost all interest for the past experience, but it is slipping beyond my concern for everything as it was.

There is no distance between us. I can feel as close to you now, even closer, than I ever did or could in earthly form. My action and behavior toward you both was not kind at one time. Please forgive me . . . no, you have forgiven me. I send this just to let you know how sorry I was for years spent in total ignorance.

Marie is a good strong soul. She can prove helpful to you, as I should have been in the cause you are presenting.

The reason I cannot give you more details about the Krugerrand is because I have lost interest in all earthly things and matter, so that my spirit and energy cannot conjure up enough power or interest to inform you further.

August 17, 1983 / 11:45 p.m.

Hi! This is Katy,

Believe me, this is a time which I have reserved to say something in confidence to you, which I would not let anyone know in public. You are performing a feat which is really trivial and yet equivalent to many experiences you have had.

You see, Wallace, your consciousness is much like mine — at least it was. You are superstitious as well as envious of those in power. I have watched you and observed you — at least while I have been in this new embodiment.

You have much to give and are giving it to the highest level of which you are capable at this moment. You have many great talents and abilities to give. Yes, I am critical of you at this moment. Your behavior is not conducive of your high office nor to your true potential. You must remember, you came out of a climate of religious orthodoxy which is most confusing to today's world.

Josie has asked you to relate my knowledge of the

Bible. I have not encountered any evidence or fact as to the reality of the entire experience as related in the Bible. I have not evidenced, nor seen, nor experienced anything which the Bible portrays or relates. We are doing our own thing and seem contented in it all.

I am not being specific in fully answering Josie's question, but I can assure you that there is much truth in what the Bible portrays, but there is no evidence to the actual dates happening as it was recorded.

I will fill you in later as to the fulfillment of this question.

God bless you, Katy

I am not finished. You have opened a new can of worms, so to speak, that needs more complete answers. I am not qualified to give you all the answers at this time. All I can say is that, at present, I have no knowledge of the whereabouts of Jesus or the intended God of which we often spoke.

This may all sound strange to you, and I am not suggesting you change your form or strategy. You must realize there has been a tremendous time lapse between the time the Bible was written, and the world today.

You asked me to help you, and I am quite willing. I seem to be coming in very strong to you at this time, but it is extremely necessary. You have already seen some, and can see more, steps to alleviate the discrepancy between things taught and reality. I continue to be your friend and guide. The fact that you are transcribing this message is evidence of that.

Continue to be true, to be strong, to be loyal and most important, to believe not only in the things I transcribe to you but also in the things you already know in your heart of hearts.

That is all for this time. Remember, I am your friend and choose to be your guide. The rest is up to you.

Good night and good living.

Signed, Katy

August 23, 1983 / 4:30 p.m.

Hi! This is Katy,

I am ready to speak if you are willing to listen. What I have to say may be interpreted in an unfriendly fashion, but I mean it for good.

You expect so much of Truth to work for you, but you are putting up a battle just as others are on the human plane. I am so aware of your depression, because it opens old wounds within me that I need to forget and overcome. You must remember that what appear to be new problems and setbacks are not really new. They were started by each of us long ago, but we have not bothered to really do anything about them. I am so familiar with this episode. There are no new problems — only unfinished business that has to be worked out. This is where our learning experience is necessary. Josie has more knowledge of this than you.

I am not angry with you, only disappointed and a little disillusioned. You speak the Truth so authoritatively, and I know you think you believe what you are saying, but you *must* be consciously aware of what you are saying, thinking and believing — not just giving lip service!

You are surprised and shocked at what I am saying to you. I understand that perfectly, but this *must* be a lesson to you, and if I am to help you, this is the method I have chosen.

You may question as to how I know this or can relate it to you. Remember, I passed over here leaving a human heart with two holes in it. *(Note: medically labeled atrial septal defect)*. Here are two vacant spots, hollow spots that were in my emotional nature. This was a vacuum where there was no love — empty. I spent a lifetime feeling sorry for myself, creating an even greater vacuum. When I am aware of the emotional emptiness you have been experiencing, it triggers off old emotional scars, which does, at least yet, produce a wearisome feeling. I am having to work out of this, and you could be of help, if you would hold to the lines, as you should, and be the real comforter that you are capable of being.

You came into this world with much of the same discomfort I had. It will not affect you as it did me, but you must remember the leakage of the heart you endured. Your love was leaking, but you have repaired the leak. Mine was drained.

What I guess I am trying to get across to you is: "This world that you know is not real." You intellectually know that and have been so ensnared with the appearance of things that it has robbed you of its true meaning. Why do you suppose you got into Truth anyway? Why does the *Course of Miracles* mean so much to you? It is every word true, and you are only afraid of discovering it *is* true, and are reluctant to accept it.

You have a big bridge to cross. It really isn't as huge as you think. It is *just to know* your oneness with God and quit trying to make things be as you think they should be. Stop planning ahead what you feel is right or wrong, and just accept what is happening as a learning experience, which is only what it is.

The only line I draw with our communication is not to feel or receive your negative output. I faced those very emotional fears and storms all my life. I do not need that any more.

You got the feeling that I was saying "good bye". In a sense I was, and after relating this to you, I feel much better. You must remember, over here we all feel your pains and hurts. It really isn't encouraging to us, and we also need a more majestic and enlightening experience.

Anyway, some of my old, miserable self sprang up and once again, it reminded me of my old miserable self.

Your purpose is not to inflict pain on yourself or anyone else — not that you are trying to, but that you just are. Thoughts are powerful. Let's just send each other love instead of fear. OK? Good. You will hear from me later.

August 30, 1983 / 4:20 p.m.

Hi! This is Katy,

There is no better time than now to continue our discourses. You have many questions which I will endeavor to answer. Probably one of the main discourses which I wish to discuss with you is the business of love and marriage. Either of these two, as you think of them, is correct in your human calculations. You received part of this when preparing for your last wedding. It was my energy, reaching out with this ceremony of love, as interpreted from our dimension. I was presenting it to you strongly, as you were aware, but did not identify myself.

Let me see. First of all, I would like to reveal love from our plane as we observe and understand it. There is not the personal involvement or attachment as you on the earth plane understand this. Jealousy, envy, competition, possessiveness, and resentment, as you understand them, have no part of real love. It, too, is omnipresent. Whenever there is personality, or as you would interpret it, ego identity, love ceases to exist.

Love has no part of ownership or possessiveness.

Everyone on the human plane has this as a crutch, so to speak, that gets them all tangled up in an involvement. Love is not involvement, ownership, or a corner on anyone, or anything.

Love is like the air we breathe. It is like the wind. It is everywhere yet nowhere. This is why people have such a difficulty trying to explain love or even understand it. It is nothing visible. Like the wind, you cannot catch it, capture it, envelop it or entrap it. It is like *no-thing,* yet it is all.

Here is where mortality creates the myth. It cannot be seen by human eyes or fully evaluated or experienced by the five senses.

I cannot say this is acknowledged or evidenced on all planes on this side, but it envelopes the very atmosphere where I am. You see, there are many planes or stations over here — too many to even fathom or comprehend. Each is in the area prescribed to them by their own state of consciousness. There is no such thing as liking one over here more nor less than another. At least it presides as such in the energy pattern where I am spending such a delightful time now.

You, too, could experience the same atmospheric climate as we are here, but it is much, much harder for you to do where you are than where we are. Humans have to work for it, strive for it, fight and even die to get a spark of what exists here as standard environment.

I certainly lacked on earth what I have here. You do not have to seek it. It simply is our environment. You can tap into this atmospheric sphere and feel what is our daily existence. This is the reason I romped on you as I did. You have touched it many times, but just as quickly, you reverted back to present pressures and fears, which cause you to lose contact and doubt all that you inwardly know as true and real.

Love does not happen to you, nor do you fall in love. This is a misnomer. Love does not, as it seems, come out of bodies, flashing eyes, beautiful figures or any such dazzling disguise. It just *is!* Your nature, as well as mine and everyone in the universe, is not just to love. Love is the basic ingredient of the soul and has nothing to do with the materialized composure of such things as looks, size, shape, color or sex. Such concepts will remain on the earth for many eons. It was never true of love and never will be.

I had my "big Will", who was my ego manager and helped me to promote my own identity. That is all behind me. There really is no loss, except for the ignorance that prevents us from experiencing the truth of love.

September 5, 1983 / 4:05 p.m.

Hi! This is Katy,

The easiest things to remember here are not what was said and done on earth, but those things which emerged from the glorious Self. We could allow ourselves to be so transfigured by all that we experienced on earth that it could deter us from the sublime realization of what life is actually all about.

If I could make myself clear to you, it might be this: You know I tried to make myself happy where you are but just couldn't make it. I tried, but for all the wrong reasons; I wanted to be alone, but yet I was miserable doing so. I resigned myself to situations as they were. I was lonely to some extent. I did try to push, at first, with little or no success. Will was so restless. I know I was a burden to him. I was caught in the middle of a vortex. Things I thought I would find pleasure in were not that exciting. I discovered out of loneliness what I thought I would find out of worldly experience. I know this doesn't make much sense to you, but there is a true answer. We think we know what we want and what is for our highest good; we are disappointed when things do not go as we planned. There is a plan, but humans have a way of preventing the thing they want.

As far as marriages are concerned, marriage is an institution provided and invented by man. Marriage is merely a symbol of what true love should be, but isn't the way you are experiencing it. Marriage, to the human mind, is considered a commitment, indebtedness, investment, used for security purposes. More rightly, there are no such things as marriages where we are — no commitments nor contracts. We are all entities as a unit, composed of no certain properties nor credentials. Each is a being yet not singular — there is a common purpose.

You are common to no one but yourself. You are an entity so unlike what you thought you were or think you are now. You see, relationship and experience are entirely different, yet it is all so familiar. I guess I knew it on the earth plane all along but did not know it as completely as I know it now.

Do you understand? We do live in two worlds, and each is separate and oblique to the other. It is much easier to understand the situation from this side. The old morality of marriage as necessary does not exist here, but it must apply to those on your earth plane. Even though it is unreal and not valid, so to speak, it must, of necessity, be the rule of thumb to unenlightened souls.

The symbol of marriage is so much like true union of its native nature, but one gets caught up in symbolism without understanding reality. It will be so on earth for eons yet, in a modified stage.

Disembodiment is also a strong experience at first, but as all else, our memory returns, and we discover we have not actually lost a body. We are in our original state. Just how long I will be in this dimension I do not know nor am I concerned. Everything is so pleasant here. I'll never tire of this environment nor feel lost.

Katy

September 8, 1983 / 4:15 p.m.

Hi! This is Katy,

I stood by your side yesterday, you and Josie, and listened to things I was not projecting of my own volition. Through this experience I am also learning new methods and ways of communication. This energy pattern is somewhat new to me as yet. I am aware of thought transference but was not aware of how it was transmuted by energy patterns. I can see how this works now that I have experienced the process in operation. I cannot say that I felt anyone or anything penetrating my field of thought. That is, to say in your language, anyone calling me on the phone and wanting information, or someone probing my brain for certain knowledge or facts. I know we communicate with each other here without the use of language or linguistics, as you say. The energy pattern, as I have perceived it, is like an energy bank where all knowledge is stored. This contains information of past, present and future as you understand time. All is there. Depending on the development or attainment of such souls who can elevate themselves to a high level, they can look into the future. Few are able to do this in a pure and unadulterated manner. You, or anyone who is high enough in a legitimate spirit of pure wisdom, can receive this stored knowledge. It is not only a matter of spiritual development or one who simply aspires to attain this goal. It is a matter of sitting down and trying to do so by also believing you can.

You, Wallace, for instance, should know this. How often have you wondered about, or even trusted yourself, to believe that which is possible. I simply felt so close to you, for your concern over me, that my thought patterns were arrested by your consciousness. You, too, felt this very deeply, and our wires crossed and touched.

Josie need not feel in any way slighted because she is unable to contact me. In fact, she has a beautiful way, naturally, to communicate with me and I with her. Josie is a natural with this sort of thing, but she, too, wants to check it out and be sure or certain.

I, too, felt the exalted and extended thrill of this experience. I was not aware at first as to just what was transpiring. I simply thought of you two and here I was, as I have often been.

You see, humans have a difficult time in trying to understand how such travel is possible. From our side to your side there seems, to most people, to be an impenetrable wall. It is still apparent that some over here feel this way and cannot believe such communication is possible. Those who do believe this are doing it many times, but the human mind is dull to all such transactions.

Earthlings are really unenlightened to the true facts of life and reality. I know I was, and you may be questioning yourself how this is possible. You see, I am not actually, as Katy was not, all that enlightened. I am not some angel or cherub who suddenly has developed certain abilities and can perform magic feats.

Katy, as you knew her, is no more. In one sense, I am dead — finished as once I was. This does not disturb me as once I thought it would. Yes, the Katy you knew is dead! But here I am as I have always been. It is like I was dreaming a nightmare all the time, or I should say, a lot of the time. But it was only a dream. What I am saying, to make it clearer, is that what I thought I was experiencing were pictures my mind was projecting. I, as a soul, was not experiencing or disturbed by all of this. I, as Katy, was many times disturbed and distraught. My final days on earth certainly helped me to gain what insight I have now. Read the last letter, and you will catch what I am trying to say. It, or something, did happen to Katy while on earth, but I am not that Katy now, nor was I ever that Katy. When I came to earth, I entered what you might consider a *school of life*. I needed to learn certain lessons on the earth plane, for my growth and understanding, that I could not learn here.

My inner eyes are opening more and more; while Katy's eyes were opened, she was blinded and oblique to what truly was and is.

You are on the right track. I do not say this from any ego sense, as though I am suddenly all-wise. On this side you have an opportunity of seeing the whole picture. On your side you see only half of the coin and believe that it is the only side of reality.

September 13, 1983 / 11:55 a.m.

Hi! This is Katy,

You are not alone in the decision-making that must be done. I can understand ever so well what once compounded me into thinking that my own self-sacrifice was enough. There is much to be done on the human plane and in this decision-making . . . it must come about, not through the ordinary sources of the human mind, but from a higher source of intelligence. Yes, the power seems to come from the human mind . . . but the human mind is but an instrument. It is so easy to get them tangled up and to believe that the human mind is the source rather than the higher forces.

I was close to believing this is how it operated, but after arriving at this higher dimension, I discovered that much of what I thought was true, was false. There are many levels of consciousness that must be discovered. We are so limited . . . even here to a degree, which may seem strange to you. We are actually no different from you, but much of what was hidden is now revealed. On the human plane there is so very much that is concealed, and the human is blinded by temporal powers that restrain them from seeing or understanding the full picture.

I am at liberty now to reveal to you that I was not aware of how the energy patterns worked. I had used that term, which seemed so convenient, without fully understanding its full ramifications. We here are not that totally enlightened, but we can be, just as you can be on your level. We do not have the trafficking of human thoughts to contend with as you do. We are somewhat free of all the entanglement which you are bothered with on earth. But yours is a learning experience such as ours.

Never for one moment be concerned with what goes on in your earthly enterprise. There are many lessons that must be learned, and how you as a person handle each situation determines to what extent you are ready to proceed further into higher levels of learning.

I must say to you at this time: "Be not anxious for your life . . . etc." That statement always bothered me while on earth, and I could not understand how I could be free of the fears that oppressed me. It is easy enough now to know the truth. What you are experiencing is good, and you will discover it, if not now . . . later.

Be alert to the many changes that will be taking place on your plane. There is nothing to fear in all of them. Fear is one of the deadliest quirks of the mind to deal with. This is why having faith in your inner strengths and powers is so necessary. You, like all others, are not yet aware of the full ability you have, not only to meet these new experiences, but you have the knowledge to overcome them.

I know that I was bothered with that problem, and I can well see and understand why you and all others are having such a difficult time with it. At least, you are balanced with the knowledge or spiritual energy that is coming from Josie. Never, at anytime, feel afraid to trust her judgment. You have been dubious in the past, but you are at the place of understanding where you can now see and validate all that Josie is saying.

As for Will — do not be concerned about him. I had been many times in my earthly scene. Will just needs time to assimilate and grow in this direction. He has been a businessman all his life, and his concerns are not functional on the plane on which we are operating. This does not mean he is at a lower standard. This you must realize. There is a time for everything. In reality there is no such thing as time . . . but there is that area where one must become aware of that which already is. Continue to be patient with Will. He is beginning to see some light but is far distant from the place we are operating on at this time.

You will encounter many such souls who are striving to attain this light. You must learn to be forebearing with them and try to understand where they are coming from. Does this sound at all familiar to you? It should. You have heard it many times, and it is difficult for you to grasp the full meaning of it, but you are.

September 16, 1983 / 8:45 p.m.

Hi! This is Katy,

You are living in a rapidly changing world, where everything about you is undergoing vast alterations to your style of living. I can give an account of this, for my transition from your world took place just four months before this transcribed message. I lived long enough to observe, as well as experience, attitudinal upheavals in former ways of living, giving account of all the necessary uprooting of previous patterns of thoughts, beliefs and attitudes.

Get into orb with my vibratory Spirit. Rest your mind. Do not think or extract what I am stating and do not try to change, alter or correct these statements, for I am spending the energy in correctly translating to you. Peace, peace, peace. Relax and become still and listen, for I speak truth.

K.

September 19, 1983 / 1:05 p.m.

Hi! This is Katy,

You have had time by now to assimilate all that I have given to you. There are many yet unanswered questions, which I shall give to you as the right occasion presents itself.

You are wondering about the type of earth atmosphere or environment in which we live. You imagine that we are living on a planet such as yours. This is the big mistake the majority of people make. Either that, or they believe we live in some kind of heaven as conceived by earth people.

We do live. Yes, we live in what you might call a place, but it is not a three dimensional place as you perceive . . . a place where there are objects, etc. and a ground upon which to walk. We live in a dimension of what you might call space. It is certainly not space to us, and we have no difficulty in getting around and there is much to see and plenty to do. I can very well imagine the difficulty in trying to decipher what I am seeking to explain. I would have the same trouble as you had I not known what I know now. You will just have to be content with my terminology, as there is absolutely no way of perceiving with your use of the human mind. I told you once before, that here we are not using the conscious mind as you understand it. Things here are *just what they are.*

We are like a dimension in time without the usage of paralleling existence. Now, by time, I do not mean the kind of time you refer to. Time is endless, and by paralleling existence, I mean that there is exactness here, and there is no division or separation in things appearing or things as they are. Existentialism, on your plane, is a matter of division, and there is competition existing between each object or related happening.

There is, in reality, no less of me than I once was on earth. You seem to believe that there is. People on the earth plane usually accept this as true, but it is not true. There is an extension to my being that I was not aware of on earth. The human factors enter in, and there is a blank so far as the reality of one's being is concerned. You only know part of your being and the largest part is hidden, not only from your memory, but also from your awareness that such exists.

Let there also be to you this piece of information. You have been, and will always be, the self that was created perfect in the beginning. We here have an opportunity to compare these existences. So much opens to one when they arrive here and go through the *resting period,* which is merely an adjustment from one world to another. There are not two worlds as there seem to be, but we shall relate to such in our communication. You see, without the true sense factors that we are using, you cannot see or understand. You are shadowed by earth senses, which is quite different from what I am referring.

No one who ever knew me on earth would be able to understand what I am saying or referring. I, too, was limited, as all people on earth are limited. We, here, are beyond the time barrier. We are also free of corporeal imprisonment. That does not mean that I am any better than you. You are the same right now, and so is every other human being on the face of the earth. When they arrive at this station, they, too, will discover what I have discovered.

You limit yourself, just as an embryo is limited. In your usage of time, you think of beginnings and endings, good and evil, before and after. Over here, we are unlimited by time factors and are allowed to see the entire spectrum. By entire spectrum, I do not mean those stations which are yet above and apparently beyond us. I mean that even this exists, but we need to grow and develop to find ourselves in that dimension.

You are in one dimension, and we are in another. You exist just as we exist. You cannot see me, nor hear me, and I appear to you as gone forever from your experience. This is not true. We are forever one, and nothing but time, as you know it, causes the fracture and disappearance.

Allow some of this information to filter through your consciousness, and you will begin to be able to penetrate the so-called veil that separates us. There is no real separation. I cannot emphasize this enough. No separation.

September 19, 1983 / 1:45 p.m.

I was not finished with our conversation. You seem to be in a hurry to finish, but there is more I wish to say. For your benefit, and the concern of others, this place where I am, and where other souls return, is not heaven, and it is not hell. Some of certain faiths think it is purgatory. These things are but myths that the human mind has conjured up because of its inability to relate. Certainly, there is a continuation of individuality, but quite different from what you suspected.

The peoples of the earth will have a difficult time trying to comprehend what I am endeavoring to say. Again, I wish to stress that this is *not heaven and it is certainly not hell.* The best illustration I can give at this dimension is as a *Universal Station.* There is certain evidence of people arriving and others who are departing for whatever it is they must unfold to do.

Religion on earth was not a vital part of my existence, but I did, as many others do, have certain views of what one should do so far as worshipping God was concerned. Even that which I believed to be true, is far different from what I am now experiencing.

There are no such things as worship services, prayer services or any semblance of churches as you know on earth. There simply is no need for such activities. We are immune from any need of such practices.

No one, as yet, has given any instructions on so-called behavior or conduct. You simply know what it is you are to do, and busy yourself with doing the thing of your choice. You might compare this to a university, although, to do so in your terms, might seem ridiculous. There are no scholastic standards, tests, diplomas, societies, fraternities with which you are familiar. We are all learning what it is we wish to learn. It is quite a reprieve from what we were doing on earth.

I will let you go for now. Be patient with yourself. You have many questions and doubts, but you will soon feel the energy flow of a higher consciousness, which will usher you through the corridors of space into eternity and all that it has to offer.

September 21, 1983 / 3:35 p.m.

Hi! This is Katy,

Having newly arrived on this plane, I wish to offer you and all others this prerogative. You evidence in daily life on your planet, many encounters with other people, situations and normal routine events.

Have you ever stopped to realize how much of your time is utilized in questioning these events but never seeking to understand how and why such experiences are happening? There is a definite plan in wait for each of you — a plan infinitely greater than you can imagine. Things just do not happen by accident, chance or luck. Much of your world is in a quandary, wondering why gain and fortunes come at times, while other unpleasant and unfortunate changes are taking place.

For instance, you see someone come into a fortune, and you applaud his or her good luck. Then soon you begin to wonder why such good fortune is not coming to you. In this, you find yourself in somewhat of a bind, which creates a breach in your thinking and feeling — condolence for yourself on one hand and envy or jealousy on the other. Herein, is a paradox in question. You see, there is an over-all plan not as yet revealed to you. There is a definite reason why good fortune comes to another, leaving you empty-handed and bewildered.

There is no such thing as good fortune to some and not to others. It is not due to luck or chance, but by the cosmic barometer meting out to one who has earned that good fortune, as you say it. Your time will also come, which has nothing to do with the way you worship or even think. Thinking, per se, is not the answer. Neither is a trivial prayer for some desired good, just as you are well aware. Every worker is worthy of his hire. Some workers are paid immediately, while others appear to have a waiting period. This is not due to a lack of funds in the Infinite bank, but rather a lack of belief and understanding in the nature of universal law.

You see, one has not only to expend effort, concentration and work, but has to have an inner conviction of being one with the fount of unlimited good. There is more to receive than "your just dues," or as some say, simply, "I'm worth it." Here we find one still operating in the category of thought processes.

While you are busy with some enterprise or effort to be creative, is it simply for this reason alone or for some monetary gain? Yes, every laborer is worthy of his hire. But don't forget you are simply building collateral which is being added to your account with compounding interest. Your payday will arrive if you do not concern yourself about it or simply give up in despair as helpless.

Look at it another way. You are creating a structure, and your creative efforts are not in vain. In this, you are changing your energy field as you apply yourself to inner talents and abilities, and are constructing a powerful force field for good, which shall present itself in due time.

September 22, 1983 / 1:30 p.m.

Hi! This is Katy,

I am not trying to change your life style for any other reasons than for your discovery of your true self. There are no gains in this for me, nor are there any profits. I have completed my life style on the planet earth, and I only impart to you some of the knowledge I have gained, especially since my arrival on this plane.

I am not seeking to be a do-gooder, or to feel some inner sense of personal pride or hopeful gains. What I am saying to you is none other than the Truths that have been presented to the world from time to time by others, or I should say, higher sources. Please do not consider me as some saint or celestial being from on high. I was once just as you, and what I have discovered is the final truth about every individual. I could no more understand this at one time on earth than perhaps you are struggling to do at this time. It was not until my later days on earth that I began to see some insight to my true worth and the same goes for you.

All humans busy themselves trying to be progressive and gain some prestige and prominence . . . not to speak of personal gains that could be collected by so doing. I did not, nor do I now, take any personal pride in what little I accomplished on earth. There was a time when I perhaps thought that to attain certain goals was my chief purpose in life. But since coming here I realize that what I, as a human being, was seeking to do, was not from my own personal self, but from a higher intelligence seeking to function through me.

Each of you has such an intelligent center within yourself. Do not make the mistake of attaching any credence or credit to this being something of your own self worth. It is of your self worth, which has nothing to do with the human element. You, friend, the self of you, can accomplish much. There is no limit to its capacities and its powers. The human you is merely an instrument through which this creative energy comes.

September 26, 1983 / 3:25 p.m.

Hi! This is Katy,

In lieu of the many issues in the world today, and confronting all of the doctrinal theological theories rampant, I would like to inform you further, concerning the real life issue that is prevalent on both sides of the life cycle.

It appears we live in two worlds, one the apparent, visible world that we dwell in, and the invisible world that we assume we live in.

There are certain matters of great concern on both fronts. First, let me say, we have an existence just as you, but quite different. Many of the matters that concern you are of a materialistic nature. On this side, we do not have to contend with such issues. We have left the world that decides what will happen to us to a great extent. This may sound puzzling to you at first. You believe that you each have a life of your own to live, and an individual mind to conduct and direct your course of action. If you will pause to reflect a moment, you will discover that much of your life is not self directed or self chartered. This does not mean that you are under some destiny, plotted by another, or that you are merely the victim of some whimsical director or autocrat. Your life was chartered by none other than you, yourself, long before you ever entered the human life cycle.

On your side of life, people are so busy living out the life plan already chartered for them by their own previous decisions, that there is a tangle in unscrambling the destination that each has chosen for him/herself. We spend the time here in seeking out a life plan, and we have the opportunity of scrutinizing all the variations.

You see, some plans that are made involving other persons may conflict with the other's destiny. You have that to deal with all through your human life cycle: conflicts, opinions, beliefs, cherished dreams that are forgotten from the original plan and interrupted by some intervening of another's desire.

One must forever be on guard for outside forces imposing themselves on our inner goals of life. We are learning a trade, so to speak, on this side, that, should we return, we will have something of paramount importance to contribute to the world.

September 27, 1983 / 6:03 p.m.

Hi! This is Katy,

Something else of paramount importance needs to be considered in relationship with the September 26th communication. In regard to our study and preparation on this plane, we, at this time, have no indication of what our next project or journey will be. In fact, it is not even considered. There is a time, as you call it, spent on this plane for proper assimilation and thorough investigation of the life we just experienced.

It may amaze you, somewhat, as to how much we apparently know in this short period, that we did not know on earth. As stated previously, this knowledge or information is available as soon as we are able to receive it after we arrive. By this I mean, there is a period where the transitional adjustment must be made in what I already referred to as the *sleep state* and the *awakening*. The awakening period is truly beautiful, as it is amazing how much we discover of ourselves that was once concealed, and we all walked around as blindfolded and dumb. Frankly, I do not like the choice of the word dumb. I did not mean it in the sense of a lack of intelligence, because one can be ever so remarkable and brilliantly attuned mentally on the human plane, yet deprived of the real essence of enlightenment.

The word enlightenment is used in a different context on our plane. Even the word *light* has an entirely different interpretation. You think of light as some form of mechanical brilliance, or some visionary encounter that is operable, or natural rays of the sun. Over here, illumination or enlightenment has an entirely different value.

It is quite difficult for you to evaluate properly the usage of true light. Everything in the universe is composed of energy. Earth people are quite concerned with energy and are seeking new forms of energy, the conservation of energy, and the usage of energy. Energy is the most natural part of everything on this plane of existence, just as you are aware on that plane, while you are looking for new ways of developing energy and storing energy from different forms of matter. Here this is not necessary and everyone here is aware of what I am saying. One of the first things that I encountered is this energy and its extreme abundance and its availability as well as its permanence.

K.

October 3, 1983 / 4:00 p.m.

Hi! This is Katy,

The communication you have been receiving has been in minimal form. You have been transcribing these messages for several months, earth time, and by now you have a more expanded view of life after life. Perhaps it would be well to expand this information beyond the confined limits of a two-way communication, so to speak, between our worlds.

You on earth have many questions as to the existence of life beyond the boundary of earth-wide tragedy, on into that of future episodes. Never, in earthly existence, did I believe this was possible, and there will be those who disbelieve what is being revealed. I cannot say one can place any blame on those who disbelieve. I, too, was among the rank and file of such doubters, but toward the end of my life on earth, I became aware of a change of attitude. I was once a person just like any of you, and I can very easily understand your doubts about this manuscript — as to its being false or ill-related.

For what good you receive from these lessons, you have my sincere blessings, and the love of all who have traversed to this plane and could testify to the truth of what is stated, if it were in their power to do so. The only reason I honestly believe this communication is at all possible with me, is because of a special type of mental pattern that exists between me and the one transcribing these messages. Somehow, there was a cosmic connection that existed between us that I was not aware existed until I arrived on this plane. To call it friendship is not adequate to explain the fusion. To call it love would be misleading, for people on the human plane have yet to comprehend the true meaning of love. Love, as stated on the earth plane, is relative to the relationship that exists between father and mother, husband and wife, sister or brother, or the bond existing between parents and children.

Such a relationship continues to exist on the human plane and is not only evidenced but encouraged. Let me say there is absolutely nothing incorrect about this bond, because it is a direct reflection of the kind of love that is necessary among all peoples. We on this plane have been stripped of the human factor that scrambles for the real and pervading love that is everywhere present on this side of life and should be as active on the human scene.

You cannot help but be confused and discouraged as you observe the break-down of material love among human beings, as well as the breach in the home, family and children themselves as they seem to rebel at parental authority.

What the children of the earth are seeking is a more realistic attitude between each other — a relationship that is devoid of pretense, mockery and false assumptions.

You see, we on this plane are endeavoring not only to observe and study the relationship between human beings, but seeking ways and means of sending a more realistic level of communication of love and oneness between all the peoples of the earth.

Having an open and receptive mind is most necessary for all types of communication; not only communication between earth people, but also with communication from this and all forms of beings. Simply having a desire or drive to develop this quality of communication, say from this dimension of life to another, is not enough to make it possible. At least, I never had any glimpse or idea that such was true. The instrument through which I am communicating believed such was possible, but he too, was very slow to believe what was unfolding in him.

Therefore, these messages are for anyone who is willing to accept what is being stated. There is no right or wrong in this communication. There is no advantage or gain to me, and the channel through which I am communicating has no alternative but to gain greater insight into the old, old question: "What really happens when the soul departs from human life?" "Is there an afterlife?" "Is there a heaven or hell which souls go to when they have terminated their life on earth?"

It pleases me to know that the time is expanding when many, many more will begin to see the value in understanding.

K.

October 3, 1983 / 11:30 p.m.

Hi! This is Katy,

Energy is the life force of spirit that gives vitality to all existing things. You have the belief that all form, in and of itself, is self-sustained. There is a vast difference between things formed and things created by the Infinite Source of God, which is an existing field of energy.

You are now aware of the tremendous force you are evidencing and experiencing on the earth plane. It seems apparent that this force field is out of kilter, and that you are threatened on every front by the existing dangers that seemingly await you.

Such is true, but there is one exception. The energy you are witnessing is only a pilferage of the true and authoritative force field that is in readiness of expressing the enormous degree of good that is intentionally, determinedly prescribed for you.

October 13, 1983 / 12:00 Noon

Hi! This is Katy,

Wallace, this message is specifically directed to you, and to any others who are prone to look on life in such a very personal manner.

It is difficult, I know, to completely release a friend or loved one from the human sense of values. You will remember, once before, I explained to you that I am no longer Katy as you knew Katy. I realize how difficult it is to erase from the human mind all memory of one you formerly knew. Yes, I am me, but not the Katy you have long entertained in your thought. I appreciate your concern over my former beliefs and feelings, for it shows you're remembering me and your deep concern over my well being. Well, that episode of my life is over and complete.

What is transpiring is more concern with your attitude and beliefs about yourself and me, but this is where we must lose all dependence upon crystallized thought forms and impressions that we have tenaciously held for so long. I realize you are remembering me as I was rather than what I am. This, you know, can interfere with our communication. You must have a free and open mind that is not cluttered up with personal thoughts or feelings. Many, many human beings live too much in the past. I can say this with certainty, because I was such a person and have no intention of criticizing or finding fault. This is a part of my former human experience of which I wish to be rid.

Those on the human plane who have a problem dealing with emotions are easily swayed and convinced that they are correct. It does indicate a concern, but one which is detrimental rather than correct or uplifting. This is where people who are emotionally involved with life in the form of politics, religion, or personal concerns of the heart, insofar as human relations are concerned, are easily upset and deeply disturbed. I want you to know that this kind of thinking and feeling can truly rob you of the true insight and cause a major effect on the human body, as well as other humanly related forms of business.

Remember, it is important to take a good look at both sides of the coin. There are two sides to every problem. You should know this by now, as you have heard Josie speak of it enough, and again, she is correct.

Your hot pursuit of rectifying or correcting matters according to your own thought patterns is admirable in one sense, because it is one of the bonds we have and is perhaps one of the reasons these communications are possible. You are a sincere student of Truth and know many things. Your suspicious nature is not dangerous and can cause you no real harm, if you will only listen closer to your inner self that can and will direct you into the correct path.

Believe me, this is not singularly directed to you alone. This is for all people. You have an excellent opportunity to help others to correct their mistakes and to get on the true path. This also applies to you, and it is because of our special type oneness that I bring this to your close attention. It is not only beneficial to you, but will awaken you in your understanding of how to relate and communicate, as well as to counsel others.

In this, we get into the area of certain inner convictions that humans select for themselves, such as opinions and fixed beliefs that are often unfounded, all of which deprive us of gaining clear vision and true insight. I was once a very opinionated person and now understand just how depriving that is to one's well being. This, to a degree, applies to all humans to a variable extent. Some can handle such situations much easier than others. These are some of the things people attract to themselves to overcome.

One thing is certain . . . I was a late bloomer but am thankful that I made a partial transition from this state before I left the earth plane, otherwise I would not be ready to continue my unfolding in such an easy manner. I say easy, because not everyone over here is able to climb this particular ladder as easily as I have been able to do.

October 17, 1983 / 1:30 p.m.

Hi! This is Katy,

There are some things better off said than unsaid. Then, there are other times that warrant definite explanations without revealing too much content of the subject in consideration.

Some people have a habit of remaining too confined in their thinking and never allow themselves to be obvious enough in searching just what it is that is going on in their inner feelings. I am indeed glad at this time that your mind is open enough to receive what it is I have to say. There are times when you have an inkling of what is coming, but today you are wondering just what it is that is being stated.

People think they know what another person is thinking and feeling. Too much assumption is credited falsely to this alibi. It is just that . . . an alibi. The average human mind is too opinionated and unwilling to be open and receptive to both sides of a situation. There is one thing most sacred and precious to every individual and that is the privilege of concealing one's thoughts and beliefs. Even though an individual feels he is fully explaining his or her innermost thoughts, there are some things that are omitted and eliminated. This is why there are some things better off said than unsaid. Then, there are those things which are better off unsaid than said.

The human mind has a protective screen which prevents too much inner self analysis. This does not mean that one is to keep such introspection secret from his or her self. Usually we only allow our communication to be stated in certain bounds in order to prevent too much to be stated that may be revealing.

From this side, we are learning the real value of inner reflection, honest approval and evaluation of those things which we have kept concealed within ourselves while on earth. It is not that way over here. Of course, we are not faced with the same temptations or illusions on this plane which you are experiencing on your level.

Over here such things as pride, fear, contempt and temptation are eliminated from one's thinking. Never, for one moment, believe that we here are unable to think and reason. Quite the contrary. We are open and exposed to all manner of the feelings we had on earth, and we have the privilege of searching out reasons, not just excuses.

You see it is absolutely important to understand why an individual is thinking and feeling as he/she is. Much thought comes as opinion, other thought comes through adolescent training and through experiences that are not too clearly discerned. While encompassed within a human body, there is too much interference from the external sense of world to allow an individual to do any real or sincere contemplation of comprehension.

I wish to emphasize once again that this place, where we are, is not heaven as thought of by the peoples of the earth. What lies beyond us here is just as much a mystery to us as it is to you — the difference between your world and ours. Everyone has his/her own concepts or theories, but to be able to sit down and comprehensively review and explain what the so-called *other side* is like, is simply an impossibility. Impossible to understand, that is, until we arrive at that destination.

I honestly believe we here have a greater perspective of what lies ahead than you on earth. The reason for this is that you believe that where we are now is the ultimate heaven. It would be impossible to get everyone to understand this difference. *Here is where some things are better off unsaid than said.* It is good, however, to have an open ended mind where the individual can explore regions that are beyond the known. In a sense, I am a newcomer to this new environment. There is much to learn, and it will be some time before I can get a better insight as to our real purpose for being here. This is not the destination of the soul, although many here honestly believe this is where they will remain forever and ever. This I know is not true. There is a continuing from here into much, much higher dimensions, and according to our spiritual unfolding and qualifications, will we be able to transcend this station to even higher ones.

Sorry you were interrupted from our conversation, but I believe all I had to say in the beginning has come forth in an orderly and sequential way. Be sure you keep your lines of communication open, for you never know when I will drop by for another conversation. You see, Wallace, this is not just a one-way conversation. You believe you are simply listening to me and have nothing to say in the matter. As a matter of fact, I am aware of your questions and searching, and have the ability to tap in and answer. We have a two-way communication system.

K.

October 19, 1983 / 10:58 p.m.

Hi! This is Katy,

Let it be known, herewith, that there is no such thing as death. The entire human race is caught up in the belief that a child is born and continues on through life until that final act of separation, which is understood as death. From all human appearances and human understanding this seems to be true. Again, we find evidence here of too much dependence on things as they appear to be. In this, you will find what is termed *illusion* on the human plane.

The opening and beginning of real vision is greatly limited to those appearing in human form. If you recall, Jesus said: "Do not hide your light under a bushel." This light is the force field, or what may be termed the reality of all individuals. In human form this light force, or force field, is certainly not visible and cannot be seen with the human eye, nor can it be heard, nor properly understood from any of the human senses. All the scientific discoveries of mankind are directed in searching out the cause of existence from purely a materialistic viewpoint or discoveries only. Such a search is futile and valueless to the true well being of individuals. Yes, it is true, that human beings find much comfort and solace. True, it does prolong the human side of a person's nature, but this is not the true or real direction people should seek to follow.

The inner powers and energy forces becoming known to mankind are the beginning of the real secret of all life — not just human life, but the fulfillment and reality of the individual. You will be hearing more and more about this source; it is the beginning of a breakthrough in the higher dimensions of life.

Too much time and effort is employed by earthlings attempting to discover the secrets of life. The secrets, or Utopia, for which they are searching can only be found in direct causes, not in mingling with effects or trying to correct the human element.

The only recourse people on earth have of looking into the archives, as they think of it, is their dependence on religion or some form and type of God. I know this was my problem, and it caused me to be extremely opinionated. Not that I had discovered any secrets from that approach as I was not that religious. It was something of a comfort zone that brought me temporary pleasure and security.

I wish to clear up a situation that may be of interest to you. I feel the need to impress upon you that I am nothing, nor anyone special, nor have I any powers greater than anyone else, to be able to make these communications. I wish it were possible to convey to others the ability to receive such, what I call, informative information.

Many people on earth simply go to mediums or spiritualists to find out how their dearly departed ones are doing and how they like their new environment. Such never did appeal to me. It seems to hinge on too much of a personalized humanization. Something such as we are doing in our communication may seem to many like spiritualism, or some fantasizing display of the occult, or mere witchery. No, indeed. This has nothing to do with such matters. It is an every-day occurrence; if one only knew just how closely associated we are with you, they would clearly understand. Now this close association has nothing to do with the human doctrine of personal relationship. You see, a better way to explain it is that we are not interested or concerned with the human way of life as you see it or understand it. We are not as once we were. Our chief interests and aims in life are not socialistic, economic, political, or even religious. Nor are we philosophers seeking to understand and explain the mysteries of the universe. We are of an entirely different dimension wherein there is no attachment to the earth. Now when I say this, I cannot include every soul that is here where I am appearing. There are as many different sections and divisions of life here as there are different atmospheres and societies in human life.

Every one here, as on your planet, is a potential *being*. Just as you are discovering, no two individuals on your plane see, think, act, or believe alike. Certain groups form together with like minds and find some kind of companionship or social agreements. But, at the same time, each of these individuals has within them a sovereign plan of the great Universal Being. This dimension is where the problems of human life are for the individual to work out certain patterns so that they can climb higher to their divine potential.

There are many woes and calamities on the human side. Some are good, and some are unpleasant, and some even seem disastrous. This is merely a schooling needed by each entity. The reason these experiences are being evidenced by human beings is because they are so caught up in the human field of life that they are blinded as to the real cause and meaning. You think of them as forms of temptation. And you are quite right. Human beings all have a free will. It is up to no one but the individual to carve out for himself the kind of life he wishes to live. Many will deny this as untrue. Their reasons all seem valid, because they will say, "I never chose this type of experience."; "I did not wish this to happen."; "I did not ask for this disease." And on and on the statements and complaints are made. Some will say, "Well, these are the chances you take." Others will blame it on the devil or upon some friend. Others, feeling such pressures, will seek out a god whom they believe is visiting all these tribulations upon them.

In dire desperation, many will cry out to God or something they feel is higher than themselves. They race through many various forms of what they believe will render help, such as different types of prayers, amulets, forms of wizardry, rituals and etc. What we are discovering is that all such approaches, although temporarily helpful to some, are not the answer. The answer lies only in the individual and what it is they are truly seeking.

Some people are seeking through forms of depression, illness, calamity and even death — not really understanding they are seeking at all. You would be surprised at the number of people who bring problems upon themselves, without claiming to do so, just to prove either their own self worth or for some unimaginable pleasure. This is perhaps the most difficult of all to understand. People are saying, "Why would anyone in their right mind choose to be unhappy, miserable, or ill?", "I want to be rich, happy, loved, and successful." True, this is the real desire of the inner Spirit, but having lost the awareness of this side of one's self, the drive becomes external and then one is caught up in a whirlwind of complications.

We will come to a close in this communication which opens a new door to understanding. I have information for you regarding the feed-back that exists between us. We shall continue later.

K.

Saturday, October 27, 1983
1:30 p.m.

(No "Hi! This is Katy", but the message explains it.)

Loved ones and friends, your presence here today is far more, and infinitely greater, than a mere observer or attendant at a wedding ceremony.

Your very presence is vital to this spiritual service and to this bride and this groom.

They have their minds and hearts at other places than here. They are bringing together their life dreams, aspirations and desires. You cannot hear them, nor know them with any intelligent degree, for you have your own perceptions of their lives, and hopefulness of renewing and reciting your own thoughts and dreams.

Simply stated, you are giving them not only your love and sincere blessings, but your being here indicates you are giving your energy, strength and support of this union.

TO THE BRIDE AND GROOM

Bride, _____, Groom, _____.
This is the moment, hour and day you have been waiting for, for a long, long time. If true love has brought you before us this day, cherish and remember this esoteric feeling! Your hearts and minds are filled with one of the most excellent feelings you have long treasured and in this moment's act, those dreams become a reality.

You each have much to give each other. You have hidden talents and potentials that can be ignited by this union and brought forth for the world to see and all to benefit and profit.

Guard very sacredly this love which has caused you to completely alter your lives and to start out together in a new and pioneering direction.

There may come days when you feel subjected, depressed and even isolated from the old you. But in your togetherness, you will gain new strength and creative abilities that will brighten and strengthen what you call your separateness, but this is due to the culmination of your togetherness.

Nothing will be lost. Each new experience is a gain, a thrill, a step forward and upward. You have allowed God's love to shine forth in you and reveal Itself.

Tuesday, November 3, 1983
1:00 p.m.

Hi! This is Katy,

This is a reminder or follow-up of our last communication. We are into the matter of what permits our communication between two worlds.

This is a problem of exact communication due to personal situations on your side that prevent a clear contact. Human beings are forever into many earthly experiences, which is natural, but disrupt the flow of messages that are possible.

Not everyone is able to hear the message at the present time. As stated, this is due to certain distractions that take place in your realm, and, also, because of certain belief factors that interfere with the receipt of a clear message. On our side it is extremely difficult for earth people to fully comprehend or understand our nature. We have situations to meet, but they are entirely different here than it is with you on earth.

Believe it or not, we are able to transport ourselves anywhere in time or space that is within our capacity. Now, by capacity, I mean within our ability or level of understanding. The same thing exists on the earth plane as it does here to a degree. On earth, each individual is in a different state or level of understanding. Each individual has the potential to reach the zenith, but not everyone is at that level of unfolding, wherein he or she is able to perceive or comprehend these levels. A child, for instance, is not aware of the capabilities and talents latent within at an early age. Only time and experience, as well as growth and understanding, will reveal to those individuals their true inner abilities. Some live on earth and hardly touch the inner powers within them. Others go to great heights, but there is a limit which can be reached on the human plane.

The problem is due to the necessity of caring for, and coping with, the nature of the human body. Demands are made in a physical way that we do not have to deal with, nor are we confined in this state.

Human consciousness at large is obstructed in the belief in earthly existence, and heaven or hell which comes later. It is very important for peoples of the earth to get the facts about these divisions. There are no real walls or partitions that separate one from another.

First of all, heaven is not what the average person understands or truly knows about. It is not a place where so-called *good people* go, nor is hell a place where so-called *bad people* go. From your vantage point, you think of good souls as all going to heaven where they will abide for eternity. It is, so to speak, a heaven compared to your earthly domain. Where we are is like a Way Station where souls, as you call them, come to rest, study, learn, and grow to much higher levels. There is absolutely no limitation as to the height one may attain. We here have the opportunity to learn certain lessons, whereby we can profit by our mistakes as well as our gains.

November 15, 1983 / 4:35 p.m.

Hi! This is Katy,

As an entity no longer of your earth planet, I would like to remind you and all the people of the earth system, regardless of race, creed or any form of personal, prescribed, adopted, or inherited religious belief, whether secular or philosophic, that you need not worry nor be concerned with the whereabouts of life on this side. All the people of the earth are curious, concerned and question so-called *after life*. Some are afraid, some have a certain set of fixed beliefs as to what will follow earthly existence. Some are skeptical, others pretend not to worry or to be concerned. Believe me when I tell you, and all human beings, that you will be very much surprised and even pleasantly astonished at this next meeting place.

You, yourself, Wallace, will be greatly and joyously surprised, even though you have spent your life in search of the secrets, have an open mind, and have learned much about both believing and teaching the fearlessness of death.

I reiterate, there is no death! I have mentioned this to you at other times. This cannot be emphasized enough.

A veil covers the mind of all human beings who are born on earth. This so-called veil prevents humans from remembering pre-existence, even though they seek such methods as mediums, trances, spiritualism, hypnosis or any other human method to prove there is a hereafter. Believe me when I say no one comes close to perceiving or understanding what it is like.

Take yourself, for instance, as I come into your mind while I am speaking to you. You periodically hesitate for a moment, questioning, wondering if what you are transcribing is actually happening, if what I say is true, if this is merely your imagination at work, or if this is merely an idle dream. I can assure you that every word you write is true, is coming from me, and is not of your own imagination.

You think I am dead. You were present to witness my death in the hospital. You conducted my funeral service. You saw my body in the casket. You looked at my body with sorrow. You did not recognize me while I stood at your side at the funeral service. You saw my body, but you did not see me as I am now, as I always have been and will be. You did not recognize me, because you were looking out with human eyes.

I could look into your heart, as I have many times since. I could feel your grief, which was of little surprise to me even after our years of misunderstanding. I filled your mind then, as I do now. You received my message shortly after I made my transfer, as you will remember. This was my assurance and signal to you that we were able to make a contact, a bridge between two worlds, as you say it.

Even as I speak to you now, I am standing right beside you. Now you need not look around expecting to see some materialization, or apparition. I am as I always was. Now by this, I do not mean the Katy you saw and knew, nor is this the Katy I lived in and knew. My vision, mentally and spiritually, was blinded by the curtain or veil that prevented each of us from knowing each other or ourselves.

I know you have to leave, but please take the time to listen to more that I have to reveal.

November 21, 1983 / 4:01 p.m.

Hi! This is Katy,

Put off your reasoning; put on your listening mind and I will once again flood your mind with further knowledge.

You and members of the earth plane are prone to accept and believe what is proven to you to be true. However, much discretion should be used before any sense of judgment is formed. Tidal wave after tidal wave of impressionable images present themselves to everyone for acceptance or rejection. You do not have to stop and count the number of times you have formed opinions without first checking it out to see if it is true or false. Such decisions about many matters of life can be proven incorrect instead of leading one to higher conditions which are truly correct.

Take, for instance, the matter of so-called death, whether it be sudden or over a period of time. The belief factor immediately begins its work of proving that death is a concluding matter. You and I know different, yet there have been times when we only thought we knew and understood without seeking further explanation or clarification. We immediately applied our given facts, so to speak; the edge which prohibits us from seeing any further.

Ask yourself, for instance, are you really interested in knowing what transpires when there is an apparent ending of human life? About all you have to go on is what you have accepted as true, and that is contingent on what you have been told, what you have read and what you can see. Let me assure you that it is impossible to die. I am not saying no change has been made. Certainly a change has taken place, but there is no severing of life. Such is impossible.

November 29, 1983 / 11:01 a.m.

Hi! This is Katy,

The course of life changes many times, but Life itself never changes. You will notice in your world many changes of seasons, hues, colors, environmental differences. This I discovered very emphatically in my paintings. I became aware of the many environmental changes, changes in my own moods, emotions and attitudes. Yet I, the true participant, have not changed. I can see very well now the various directional changes in my life — circumstances over which I felt I had little or no control. I can understand now where I was wrong and where corrections could have been made, but I simply felt I was incapable of meeting certain challenges.

It is clear to me now that life on the earth plane is simply a school where certain lessons must be learned and applied. Most everyone uses excuses when they're not applying themselves correctly in altering their own sphere of life. Fear is the provisional cause of all efforts to evoke needed changes.

Over here, souls are freed from such earthly matters. I am as delighted now as I was when I made my transfer to this dominion. What I feared most never happened. What I cherished most on earth is not important now. All fears, regrets, bondage to earthly matters and possessions is of no concern.

My real purpose in communicating with you is to alert as many as possible to the needless concern of living on the earth plane. Yes, the earthly lessons have a very important role in the unfolding and development of the individual entity. But there is no cause for concern. The only problem areas exist so long as one retains the human form of bondage. It need not be. It is truly not real, though it seems to be apparent only as long as one continues to fuss and stew over earthly matters that are of no real consequence.

Wallace, I know you have had your ups and downs just as I did and everyone has on the human level. You are gaining great insights into the immortality and continuity of life. Josie has helped you much more than you realize. You are beginning to see this clearly now!

Such is typical of earthlings. Each one is so crowded with preferences, convictions and beliefs that are of no consequence. The one real lesson for everyone to learn is that on the human level no one is absolutely correct. Each person cherishes and protects his/her dream world of pretend and does not wish to forfeit or release these dreams. Sacred and real as they all seem to be, they are but mere shadows of the truth that is to be revealed at the time of real discovery. (Read over the beginning of this message and you will see what I mean.)

There is no right or wrong to any situation. The world fights on to protect each individual from acceptance of an idea. What is good for one person appears to be bad for another. This is merely the cause of fastening one's attention on one belief to the exclusion of all others or anything else.

December 27, 1983 / 11:40 p.m.

Hi! This is Katy,

After our brief reprieve, it is time once again to resume our conversation. You were absolutely right in assuming that I was trying to reach you, which is another indication of your neglect in listening to what I have to say. This is not intended as derogatory in any sense of the word. It is merely a reminder, which I have mentioned to you before, of keeping your mind open and not doubting the whereabouts of this information.

This is one of the depressing marks that bothers many of those on this side. Untold directional messages are sent, but those to whom the message is delivered either doubt what they are receiving or sluff it off as imagination or foolish. I can assure you that the time is right for those on the earth plane to open their minds to receive the good that is being transmitted. This transmission of conversation has been going on for countless decades, and I can very well understand the reluctance on the part of recipients to believe what they are receiving. There are those who take advantage of these mental transmissions, or see it in a negative way, or try to influence people falsely. I am patient with you, as I know this is the problem you are having at the present time. I would, too, if I were on your end of the line, not knowing what I know now.

As time progresses, you will become more assured and convinced that what you are experiencing is very real and is not imagined or self induced. The peoples of the earth need to know the truth about continuing life in its totality. Skeptics continue to exist, and many foolhardy people do their own make believe. It is essential to you, and all the people of the planet earth, to awaken to the reality of life's existence and to overcome the foolish prejudices and conventional theories that plague so many.

I know I sound very much like an authoritarian on the subject, but there are certain realities that cannot remain a secret. Everyone has the ability to tap into the central forces of intelligent life, but the illusory nature of the human being prevents them from the deeper insight into their true nature.

You have the knowledge and know-how to by-pass the human sense of reasoning and enter into the higher nature of your being. You should live in this area rather than allowing yourself to engage in too much rationalization and outer concern. Herein is where fear and worry are engaged, which prevents a clear and proper transmission of my thoughts. I strongly feel that you are beginning to become more of an outlet for the truthfulness of these messages.

You are in a position that you can be of much help to those seeking light and understanding on the subject. This should be right up your alley. That is why you are able to pick up so quickly on what I am seeking to relate. Through your teaching and classes, you will be able to properly reveal more of what is taking place on other planes of existence to students seeking the Light and understanding.

I wish to reiterate some of the things which have been expressed previously, this time with a bit more depth and insight. Life, as you on the earth know it, deal with it, and experience its many pleasures, sadness and chagrin, is merely a dream, but an important and necessary dream. This is most difficult to relate to the average person, especially those so deeply asleep that they hardly know any difference. A mere trace of this recollection crosses their minds but is blurred out of existence by the fantasies of the world. If you but stop to think, is it possible to believe all that any of you are experiencing can make any rhyme or sense? Hardly! This thought crosses your mind many times, but is immediately erased by more external confusion and inner conflict. "The world seems so real," many will proclaim and go right on with their fantasies. I should know, as I too, was among the throng trapped in a mental world of contempt. Now I know differently and wish to convey this message to all of you who are caught up in the snares of ignorance, superstition and disbelief.

What you on the earth plane are experiencing is real. It is real to your thought existence. How is it possible to say it is not real? Sure it is real — until one awakes from the dream and discovers its unreality.

Now let us get back to the real business of our joint meeting of the mind. There is no doubt but what the earth is going through critical times. There has been a relaxing of moral and ethical training. We cannot consider this a sin but an act of violation of the law of being. You see, there is a Truth about everyone that up to now has not been publicly recognized, taught or accepted. There is going to be an intense search on the part of many people to discover the real cause of anxiety and stress. Already it has begun, but as yet, it is in its infant state. The beliefs about the self and the world have not been properly understood. You might say human beings are now in a transitional stage in which they are beginning to awaken to a long undiscovered reality.

There have been countless violations of the Truth of Being. To encounter the real problem does not mean that society at large has to search and investigate in the outer realms. It is much more difficult, of course, to enter and engage in some internal introspection. The need to become aware of one's true existence depends upon the length of time needed to encounter the horrors of human existence until such time that the individual has had enough and decides to make a change. Help will naturally be needed by all to receive instructions, heretofore, sheltered.

Human beings are not so much afraid of living in the world as they are fearful that there is really nothing else to look forward to in the future. To them, there is no real future — this dismal picture merely impedes any worthwhile reason for existence, with no hope or promise of betterment to come.

I emphasize the need for understanding the comparison of *life* as you know it from *life* that is to come. This in no way necessitates the giving up of what you know as human life, nor does it require sacrifice of any kind. How many people on the earth plane have any true understanding of what life is all about? They look upon life as simply trying to squeeze as much activity as possible in a short period of time. Life is a continuous thing. It is not a continuation of things as they appear to be with all the worthless experience and a few joys sprinkled in. Life, as it really is, has never been searched out nor discovered. That which is called *living,* as known and understood by earthlings, is hardly the correct definition. This type of experience is merely the surface trappings and scarcely resembles what true *living* is all about.

December 28, 1983 / 2:02 p.m.

Hi! This is Katy,

For our discourse today, I would like to discuss with you the subject of differences. Examine, if you will, the similarities in extensions of opposites. There are similarities in differences, just as there is likeness in extremes. Viewing these opposites from a purely effectual position, this does not seem to be true. When reference is made, however, to polarities, we discover quite another perspective.

You will notice on the effect level, or from the materialistic viewpoint, that there is quite a difference between hot and cold, light and dark, good and evil.

Let us first, for example, consider the subject of hot and cold. "Quite opposite," you may postulate. Yes, speaking from the effect level, we will all agree this is true. Ah! Let us observe closely the real nature of such opposites — and they are extreme indeed. On the other hand — neither is better or worse than the other. Heat can produce a stroke, it can parch, burn and extinguish. Likewise frigid conditions can cause frost bite, burns and other damaging effects. The results are not really different in their unpleasant effects.

Now let us observe the similarities in such differences as light and darkness. One cannot look with naked eyes into the blazing sun without blindness being produced. Yet without the light of the sun or some other luminosity, one remains blind and cannot see.

Shall we now consider the matter of good and evil? If you had all the good in the world for yourself, you would perhaps be hysterically elated for a while, but soon your Midas touch would produce fear and hate — fear you may lose your touch, fear of deception, fear some competitive force could mar your riches; hate would soon be evident, for there would be nothing more to attain. Enjoyment for such good fortune would soon wane and insanity would mark the end.

At the other end of the spectrum is a total opposite of the good, which we shall call evil. Its mark is already made, and there is no need of any discussion on this matter.

You see, my friend, while we may choose our preferences over these differences, each in its own term is equally disastrous and destructive as the other. In seeking to select the climate each wishes to pursue and enjoy, there is a need for clarification and reflection on our ideals. It is not a matter of what you have or do not have — it concerns what you *are*.

On the human plane, having things seems most desirous and necessary. One does not desire liquid when he is not thirsty, or a meal when there is no appetite. The point in consideration here does not really concern having or not having. Take a close look at the human scene. There are those who do not have things but want them, then there are those who have things they do not want. Equally, each circumstance is as offensive and disturbing as the other.

February 2, 1984 / 12:07 p.m.

Hi! This is Katy,

You have a subject for this Sunday, February 5th, titled "We Ought To Be." You are on the right track so far as the title is concerned but just what is the issue? Everyone agrees that *we ought to be,* but what is it we are supposed to be? That question introduces many wandering thoughts and desires. This subject requires much deep insight as to the reality of being. Everyone on the earth plane believes that what they are experiencing is real. What they are experiencing may not be to their pleasure, but on the other side of the spectrum, there are those good things happening to people which they can hardly believe. Strange, isn't it, how the underprivileged thinking people believe that something is *too good to be true?* That leads us to the question of what is real and what is true. Going back to the normal way of earth thought — one simply states that what is happening is true. All earthly situations and experiences are perceived as true. They may be pleasant or unpleasant according to the way a person believes or perceives it to be.

Let us ponder a moment on the subject "We Ought To Be." You may think temporarily that you shouldn't be where you are, or situations are happening to you that you think should not be. Humans say they ought to be healthy, they should be happy, prosperous, wise and the like. It would undermine their dignity, pride, or belief system to tell them they already are what they *Ought To Be.*

As we examine this statement we must have more clarification. *Ought to be* or *should be* is one side of the coin. Those who make such statements do not honestly know *what* they *ought to be.* All they are aware of at the moment is that they are not manifesting what they would like to manifest. No one on the human plane is completely satisfied or fulfilled. Is this due to the fact that they are unfortunate people, or that they are being deprived of what they think they want?

It always appears that human beings are never completely satisfied with what they have — always wanting more than they think they have. The feeling of insufficiency or incompleteness seems to plague the human instrument.

We are conversing on two opposite sides of Being. You are in human form and I appear to you to have relinquished my human form. You may even think that I *ought to be* where you are or even go so far as to say you *ought to be* where I am. Here we are talking about dimensional places, time, embodiment or disembodiment. Would it surprise you if I were to say that we are *not* actually in different zones or places? To all human appearance and belief this is untrue, and why is it that one cannot accept this fact? The reason is that you and the peoples of the earth are dwelling in the belief of time, location, embodiment, etc. While wearing the human form, one has to transport that form from one place to another. The form to which I am referring is the body. Here is another belief that prevents one from realizing the truth. "What body?" you will retort; "Why the very body I am wearing at the present." Would it surprise you to know that I, too, am in form and body? Just because you cannot see it with your human eyes does not mean that I do not exist. If I were to go away on a vacation while residing in your planet, you would be unable to see me. You may say "That is different". How is it different? I am communicating to you right now, but you cannot see me with your human eyes. Where do you suppose this message is coming from? I must have some kind of form to enable me to transmit these truths to you. I continue to have faculties with which to see, hear, move and have being. Just because you cannot see the form in which I exist is not indication that I have no being.

If we go back to this subject, "We Ought To Be," I reiterate that I am now what I am, and you are now what you are. There is completion in what we are, although we may not be aware of or expressing what it is *we are.* On your earthly plane, you are more concerned with what you are, which is related to existence, possessions, station, environment, and accomplishment.

The Truth is, we really do not have anything to accomplish except what we believe we are to accomplish. Truth is *now.* Existence is *now.* Everything exists in the now, but earthlings live in time indexes in which there seem to be separation. Remember when I said to you formerly, "The customary time in which you perceive or calculate time is incorrect. Measure it by time impulses?" *Exact time is a matter of sequential difference.*

Yes, from the human perspective you think in time rather than in eternity. You feel incomplete. You believe you are not being what you were made to be. The Truth is that you *are now what you ought to be,* only you are not aware of it as yet. There is absolutely nothing to accomplish or become, other than what you are *now,* but this fact is unknown to you.

What we *ought to be* is fully aware of who we are *now* — not will be in the future. *Now* are you alive, *now* are you wise, *now* are you love, *now* are you infinite and complete. This may sound rather strange to the majority of people on the earth. I might add that you knew when you arrived on the earth plane what you were going to be and what you were going to experience. You do not remember such episodes passing through your mind but such were true. You know right now what you are going to be, not realizing that you are *already* what you *ought to be.* Time, as you are aware of it, separates you from what is, and you believe that as time progresses you will become that thing. Time is only now, slowed down or speeded up. It has no meaning at present, but the time will come when you will be aware of this Truth. Now, when I say the time will come, I am speaking of time as known on the earth plane. Where I am, there is no awareness of time. We just are. This applies to you, but through the sense factors, the real truth is veiled and reality unknown.

K.

February 3, 1984 / 1:30 p.m.

Hi! This is Katy,

In the frame of reference in which we have been discussing the element of time . . . I would like to veer off in
the direction of *reality*. This, of course, has to do with
the subject of time.

The peoples of the world are anxious and concerned
about what takes place after leaving the earth plane.
Although people do not openly talk about such a subject, there is the underlying concern and unanswered
questions. Naturally, this has to do with the interference
of what earth people call time. The same reference is
made to space, distance, differences, and form as is made
to the subject of time.

In order to prevail upon the truth of this matter, it
can be more easily explained if one will simply empty
out of the mind all thought of what was formerly believed. This naturally necessitates the matter of closing
the door of the mind to what one thinks and believes.
This is not at all easy at first and will take a while to
accomplish.

The majority of people on the earth plane are not at all interested in closing the mind to things unknown or foreign; therefore, they will not be interested in trying this experiment. The human mind is such that it tries to act like a sponge and sop up every bit of animate matter it can claim. There are those, however, whom the world calls *dreamers,* who can apparently sit and tap into all manner of ideas, and acclaim much true knowledge and information that is beneficial to the world of form as you know it.

When such a one is able to *drift off,* so to speak, from the world of animation of those things tangible, visible, and the realm of dimension, they are able to ascend into that realm of pure ideas wherein all existence, as you know it, originates. Here, this realm, which has been thought of by some religionists as the Kingdom of Heaven, is actually the dwelling place of *energy* — the source of *all.*

It is sad indeed, I know, to be deprived of the world of appearance and the tangible forms we saw, talked with, and knew. This was the experience such as I knew while in the earth form. Now that my real vision has been opened, I can understand it in quite a different way. Already, there are those on earth who are beginning to understand more clearly the eternalness of life and being. What is being stated here is not for every eye to read nor ear to hear, for they will not comprehend. Herein, is where the "light shineth in the darkness and the darkness compre-hendeth it not."

Take for instance, on the human plane, how one closes the eyes when experiencing ecstacy or some warm embrace. At that instant of what you call time, the individual is shutting out all else. If only for a moment, one truly feels the vastness of grandeur and grace; one's vision will close to all outer events just to experience a moment of eternity.

When one sleeps, or when one dreams, the vision of finite existence momentarily ceases to exist. The same is true when one kisses a loved one or embraces in some emotional way; there is that seeking to capture reality. For this reason, meditation is employed by many just for the purpose of catching a piece of the Infinite.

February 8, 1984 / 11:47 a.m.

Hi! This is Katy,

There is so much of the concealed that needs to be revealed. You have been given the opportunity of hearing Truths that have been revealed to you, but now it becomes imperative that you permit these Truths to enter your consciousness and become a vital part of your being.

As mentioned before, there is so much wisdom and knowledge available that few are permitted to enter their minds. Remember, on your human plane, the mind, as you call it, is not the source, but an instrument through which True Wisdom can flow. Earthlings are too much into appearances and are truly ignorant of the Truth that lies back of the scene. All Wisdom lies before you now to discover. Nothing is hidden and everything can be revealed. Fortunate are those who have ears to hear, but more important, are those who can become aware of what they hear and allow these Truths to become an active part of their individual consciousness.

At this moment, as you consider time, I am resting in a beautiful atmosphere of peace and splendor. We, over here, have the opportunity, at our leisure, to review our past life experiences. It is much like your watching a television screen. You can see everything that took place; it is very vivid and very real. It is not frightening nor does it produce any guilt. By the time you reach this place of unfolding, you are no longer concerned about what happened in the past. You are able to look objectively without any sense of chagrin and have the opportunity to make corrections in your way of observing your life.

Remember the time I suggested to you very strongly that you stop looking at what happened in the past and to cease from carrying over old wounds? By now you have made enough progress to understand that such was viewed by you not from the ethereal observation, but by your own standard of human sense awareness. This was not meant to be a criticism of you on my part; I was only seeking to inform you in a strong enough manner to awaken you to the uselessness of this endeavor. I was well aware of where you were coming from, and only wanted you to know there is a much better and higher way of looking at life's scene.

Please listen to what I have to say to you, and all peoples of the earth, with an open and earnest mind. You are not, and I wish to repeat, you are *not* the limited person or persons you propose to be. Underneath all those feelings of fear, frustration, guilt and criticism there is an indomitable *you* that forever remains remote from all the frustrating and confusing episodes you are encountering. Religion, as it has been taught on the face of the earth, has not taken a closer look at the action of the infinite. Religion, as you know it, actually restricts and inhibits an individual from knowing the Truth.

Actually, the God that *is*, is not being taught or experienced by human beings. This is because God is simply a word that brings fear and often panic to people. A right understanding of God is to be sought after and realized. It seems strange, my telling you all of this, because we are not being taught about God where I am, and we have never seen God — that is to say, I have not seen God nor know of anyone where I am who has encountered the Infinite. There just seems to be a feeling in the air that one knows all, but it is difficult for me to explain how we know. For one thing, I have learned that there is no need of praying over here, for there is nothing to pray for. Everything is so complete as it is. All I can say is that there is a perpetual freedom and peace. In your atmosphere you do not have the privilege of being in an evil-free environment. You are always tense or anxious about attaining or acquiring or protecting something. There is nothing to attain where I am, and there is certainly nothing to acquire. That makes us free of having to protect anything.

When I say there is nothing to attain or acquire, I should make myself clear to your sense reasoning. We are simply observing what is. There is nothing to attain nor is there anything to protect — all I can say is that I am an extension of what I am. My life on the earth plane is, to me, a living example of what it is I am seeking to explain. In the earth experience, I had the idea that it was Katy herself who had qualities, potential, talents or whatever you choose to call what you believe to be your calling. Now that I have reached a new plateau, I have discovered this never was a projection of Katy, but it was merely an extension of what I always have been, and this part of me has its beginning in the Infinite. What little I did had nothing to do with me as a person or what you may call *my qualities*. I had no qualities nor do I have now, and this is what I have discovered. This lesson is to be learned on the earth plane, as it is here.

When the people of the earth read and hear about

their *hidden potentials,* what they are speaking about is not that an individual has any qualities of himself or herself. Such potentials are merely the Great Energy Force seeking expression. All any person can do is to make of himself an instrument through which these forces may come forth in full bloom.

Now, as I am reflecting in this peaceful atmosphere, I fully realize, with absolutely no interference, that what I am and what I was is nothing more than what I have always been, but just was not aware of this great Truth.

Anyone on the earth plane can venture far if they will only take into account that as individuals, they, of themselves, have no powers. We are all extensions of the Great One, and in our ability to discount our properties as a person and see Oneness with the Source, will we be able, wherever we are, to allow great wonders to be performed.

I would simply desire to make this one closing remark. Do not believe that what I am saying makes me special or of great wisdom. What is being revealed to you is nothing more nor less than what you as a *Light* already know. This is nothing new. My purpose in transmitting to you is to inform you of what existence is like on this plane. Nothing truly exists here that does not exist where you are. It is simply easier to recognize these Truths here than it is in the heaviness of earth atmosphere. My actions in revealing what transpires here in no way makes me a great teacher. All I am actually doing is reporting to you what is going on here and what it is like, so that you may be better informed and enlightened as to the continuing life.

K.

March 21, 1984 / 2:25 p.m.

Hi! This is Katy,

The foundation for living is the prerequisite for dying. Let me explain it in this way. All human forms of life are desirous of living, of continuing on as they are appearing at this or some given time. If you will mark down any given point of time, you will discover that it can not remain the same. There are intervals between what was and what is. As mentioned previously: *Exact time is a matter of sequential difference.* This may be better stated by saying that time is continuous. It has no beginning nor has it an end. It is a continuing process. Time, as related to earthlings, comes and goes. In this you will find past, present, and, hopefully, a future.

The fear of death haunts the human mind, as it relates to some form of the unknown. Thus dividing time you have these divisions. You are only aware of the past and know little of the present. The future exists among the unknown factors, which brings fright and concern. Since all you know is related to the past, which you know happened, and you believe it to be real and true — only the past can you recognize as reality. The future only offers a dream, a hope, or an expectancy of what you want or do not want to happen.

Dying is merely a part of living. You see, right here you are dividing life from death. Living, as you know it now, is hinged only on past experiences. You expect the future to remain the same, or at least, you're expectant of better things to come. There is always the dream of getting out of the ruts and negative experiences of the past, and dreaming of the future when your ship will come in. Here you have opposites. There are no opposites in Truth. Death is not an absence of life — it is life in its fluctuating and continual flow.

As you think of me, or anyone you knew who has passed on, you can only regard them in your relationship or experiences of the past. It is difficult for the human mind to see beyond the supposed veil that separates you from them. You only remember them as they were. You never knew them as *they are.* In fact or reality they remain the same. Do not confuse yourself with your perception of them, or of your likes or dislikes of them. You did not ever know them for what they *are.* You knew them from your own frame of reference. What you saw in them was only what you saw or knew about yourself. All the so-called evils of the world are never in the world *itself.* Evil is only existent in the one who beholds the world or the people or conditions of the world.

Your belief about me as I was and am was merely a reflection of what you believed about yourself. This is true of everyone you knew or now know. This is true not in the vernacular we refer to as *Truth.* There is but one Truth. What humans call *true* is merely their present beliefs or perceptions. You are studying about this now in your Miracle Course. This is in agreement with the matters of which I speak.

Those who come into the higher forms of Truth, as illustrated in the spiritual material now being presented to the world, are able to listen and respond to the only Truth there is, or ever was, or ever will be. Many false doctrines are prescribed and suggested but believe them not. Every human being is eagerly seeking for release from human bondage. This so-called human bondage was not placed on anyone who ever lived, lives now, or ever will live. All of these human problems are self-inflicted and self-willed. This is why we say they are mere illusions that never were real. To all human interpretation and belief, these human errors and trials are real, and all humans are seeking to be removed from what they, and they alone, have projected upon themselves.

I am very aware of all the beliefs, questions, concern, fear, and suspicion of so-called death and what goes on in the continuing process. All that an individual can come up with is the examination of the past, and this forms a frame-work for what the future will be. Such is not true. This dream of an afterlife is fettered with ideologies, theories and fantasies. Never allow yourselves to be taken up with such images. Others will question: "Will I like it over there?", "Will I still be me?", "I do not want to give up my loved ones or my possessions", "All of this frightens me." I realize and recognize these very questions, for they are the same concerns and questions I myself have asked.

There are no secrets where I am. There is nothing, absolutely nothing, that is hidden from any of you. There is nothing you are not supposed to know. That which seems hidden or concealed is but the Truth. Human beings as a whole are frightened of the Truth. It is foreign to them — so they think. Within the soul of everyone is an awareness or knowing of what it is like here. This has not been concealed by the Supreme Being or by life itself. These barriers are all self-imposed. What you are experiencing now is but a dream. This dream seems so real, whether in despondent or pleasant conditions, that it appears real. Believe me, it is not real at all. If only one will enable herself or himself to silence the mind from all beliefs, good or bad, they will eventually *know*. When I say, *good* and *bad,* this causes one to sit up and want to argue. The argument consists of stalling, the giving up of the good. What you may believe to be good at one moment may turn out to be not good or incorrect. How is one able to tell what is good or what is bad? These are only opinions or desired situations or conditions at the present.

What is it to *die* except to be awakened from a dream. To *die* is merely to *live.* Remember, life is continuous. Human forms of all nature come and go, so naturally the human being believes there is life when they can see it and death when it can no longer be seen.

To live in memories of the past is to live among the throes of death. It becomes one's own memorial service in which they place themselves in the grave and are passed away. To live today is to die to yesterday. There can be no tomorrow until today is concluded. That dream of the future cannot be fulfilled until there is an expiration of today or the now. The sun will not shine for you tomorrow unless it sets today. You cannot awaken, refreshed from sleep, until you surrender to sleep. You cannot live tomorrow until you die to today. Yesterday, today, and tomorrow are merely a matter of sequential difference. What you fear about the future is merely what you purported in the past.

K.

One more important thing I wish to state. I will be with you only in the future. This does not mean that these messages will be discontinued. Ponder this carefully. This moment is here and gone, just as the past is gone. The future is the present, but that too becomes the future. This is what we are all becoming; not what we have been or what we are now. As you aspire to grow and unfold, you are becoming that which you at present are not, and thus, this is your real *being*.

March 26, 1984 / 2:55 p.m.

Hi! This is Katy,

It is possible for me to reach out to you in answer to many questions you pose. You may be wondering, "If this is so, why do I not receive an answer?" This is a simple yet complex answer to explain. I shall do my very best to explain it in terms you and others will understand.

It is not certain that the questions we receive here are truly warranted or deserving. Even on the human level many people pose questions but really do not desire a correct answer. The only answer they want to hear is that which responds to their own purposes or rule of thought.

All questions coming to us have an answer. Another reason why they are not forthcoming is because they will not be clearly understood, thus, misinterpreted. When a soul truly desires to know, the answer will come. Just because an individual asks a question is no reason they desire the correct or true answer.

There is much to convey to you, as I have mentioned

before, and it is necessary on your part to have an open and receptive mind to receive what is being transmitted. Human emotions stand in the way of clearly comprehending the Truth. Only a rare few are at the point in consciousness where they truly desire to know the mysteries of life. There has been so much pilferage of thought and mingled grandiose theories and beliefs that the world at large is not only confused but beguiled by the torrent of explanations.

The peoples of the earth are slowly going through a transitional period, wherein, they are beginning to emerge from the throes of beastliness. The earth changes are coming about in many revolutionary forms. These changes not only include hemispheric earth changes, but social, economical, political, and religious changes as well.

You are pioneering among the few who dare to seek a break through to the reality of existence rather than tread along with safe and comfortable beliefs held so rigidly by narrow-mindedness and conventional thought. The time will soon arrive when a drastic change will be evidenced on the earth plane. People of the earth are static at the moment. They seem tranquilized by some hidden force placed there by dogmas and creeds. There must be a total cleansing of the realm of human beliefs, and a period of resting is going on now so that people may adjust and awaken slowly to the new Truth that will begin to encompass the earth plane.

Your earthly concept of the crucifixion of Jesus is so mingled with untruths and incorrect information that it will be a while before these old beliefs and concepts will wear off. There seems to be a need by earthlings to cling to the safeguards and to be afraid to accept the real Truth that is being offered. Nothing is more painful for human beings than the acceptance of Truth. This is traditional, for humans are of the earth, earthly; they have no awareness as yet as to whom they really are. The truth about every human being is safely hidden away in the confines of the Inner Self, there to remain until every vestige of fear, ignorance and old beliefs are eradicated from their consciousness.

What if I were to tell you the real Truth about earth life or about the life beyond the earth? How many do you honestly know who would be interested or accept these truths? Few there be.

As for your allowing others to read these transcriptions, be assured I have no objections other than what I have already advised you. These messages are primarily for you, and it's up to your discretion who will receive them. As mentioned in my previous message, there are no secrets here which are not available to those who touch this realm. Nothing is concealed that shall not be revealed. (This was given you before.)

There is no right or wrong to be decided upon as far as who receives copies of these messages. It is merely a matter of you not being disturbed if one does not agree, or believes this is all your imagination. You, and only you, can be hurt if you allow yourself to be so inclined.

There are theories galore circulating around the earth. Beliefs and opinions and concepts swarm the human mind for acceptance. Just play safe, and do not allow yourself to be fooled by these untrue messages. This is the reason so many have turned away from this sort of relationship with the so-called *other side*. They are, as I said before, in a tranquilized state, fearful and skeptical.

When the real Truth is properly related, there may be momentary pauses in awareness, but this will be brushed aside and illumination will follow. Herein, do you find a soul who no longer wishes to be chided and will go through a period of withdrawal. This is merely the beginning of the awakening stage.

You are in a position to correctly relate the Truth to people. You have been victimized in the past and are cautious even about these messages you are receiving from me. You have that understanding of skepticism and must be patient with those who are not so quick to believe.

The only Truths you are not receiving from me are those you yourself are unable to hear. I will release knowledge to you just as quick as you are able to receive. The illumination of all humankind and the awakening of all is not kept from them by higher forces. It remains locked up, so to speak, until they are able to hear and understand.

Your last words to me in the hospital were to keep my attention on the white light. I had faith in what you were saying. I had the opportunity of enjoying and experiencing other colors, but I have you to thank for reminding me to look at only the *white* light. Perhaps this is the reason there is this rapport with you. Few would understand. Those who are ready will benefit. It is not up to me to tell you who is ready. This is something that must be decided according to the individual's divine judgment. No harm will be done either way. No harm can come from these messages. Only good can come, but as you well know, only a few are ready to receive the good that awaits them. Uncanny as it may seem, people simply refuse to accept the good that is offered them on a silver platter. This is why the Master said: "Many are called, but few are chosen." Infinite intelligence does not choose. Infinite Intelligence is for everyone. The individual simply refuses to chose to accept all that is offered.

Katy

Wallace, do not faint or lose heart. Josie is your good companion and I love her dearly. You are in readiness for tremendous growth. Only you, and you alone, are responsible for this. Good fortune is yours now.

March 29, 1984 / 1:30 p.m.

Hi! This is Katy,

I urge all of you to rejoice in the good fortune that is coming your way. The earth plane has been plagued for thousands of years with misery, misconduct, and misfortune. The end is close to the many plagues that have come your way. The Truth that is being hurled to you from a higher dimension should not be shunned or turned away. This has been the misfortune for those on the earth plane since it was first inhabited.

Each of you, individually, will be called upon to rally your spiritual forces and surge forward in ever greater emphasis to halt the onslaught of negative forces that have been so long with you. The earth hierarchies have been to blame for this charade of misfortune and have prevented the people from knowing the real Truth.

Perhaps only those who have already altered their lives from the earth atmospheric pressures of demagoguery and untruth will be in a position to understand what is being said at this time. I can assure you that the time is right for the transfer of thought from the base human ideologies to the Spiritual Atmosphere that has long been neglected and forgotten.

This in no way is intended to place more fear in the hearts and minds of human beings. Rather, it is a call to make a correction and the time is at hand for such a move to be made. You are not called upon to forsake or give up your perspectives of life and living. All that is asked is to stretch forth your energies in more explicit ways to help usher in a golden age that is beginning to surface.

Too much has been written and said about various religious complexities. All such beliefs have now been discredited and the more enlightened slant on life is being not only surveyed but discovered. The only problem with such more enlightening forms of existence is the necessity of giving up your old concepts and beliefs and being willing to accept the only Truth there ever was or ever will be.

Entirely too much emphasis on living a mere human existence is not the order of the celestial day. Living as earthlings, know it is mere survival, is not the intention of the ethereal plan. This is why the earthlings are called upon to relinquish the past and all that it stands for. The command to arise and subdue the earth was not interpreted correctly. Yes, the peoples of the earth have made great progress with their innovations and scientific discoveries, but all such efforts have merely eroded the real plan and have left nothing but devastation and deprivation.

Such a message may sound to you much like "Doom's Day talk." But this is not the case. No one from this *other* side of life has any such intention of inflicting wrath or punishment on the people of the earth. This is all self-inflicted. The major search for the peoples of the earth is *profit and gain.* Observe yourself, Wallace, how much effort you have expended in trying to bring forth the light to people. You have many souls who are truly desirous of knowing the Truth and many others who are merely seeking for some selfish profits or gain. None of these souls are truly lost. They have merely been misguided, and it is easy for them to fall away from the only Truth that can be of help and assistance to them. You, yourself, have been caught up in the temptation to seek gains that are no more than the collection of what may be termed ashes.

Certainly this does not sound like the Katy you once knew. I can assure you that it is the same Katy — but one of whom neither you nor I were fully aware. This is why it seems so difficult for you to fully comprehend what is being said. The same that is True about me is True of you and every soul. Souls are never lost; they merely make a detour which causes more pain.

Before venturing further in my message to you, I would like to explain why Josie has not received word from me. This is not because I am not close to her, nor because I have any thought of remaining silent so far as she is concerned.

Josie is an advanced soul. I assure you, she is more advanced than even she is aware. You have secretly suspected this all along, but it has taken you quite a long time to bring yourself to accept this truth. The truth is Josie can accept this in a more acceptable manner than you. What I am saying is not far from Josie's own consciousness. There is no real need to come to her directly. She already knows deeply within herself what it is I am saying. You, too, have the ability to understand many things within yourself that you alone prevent from coming forth. I know you have the desire, and I have searched your mind and heart for your intent and purpose of being in your work. You believe you have erred or failed in many ways. This is not true and you will become more aware of this as time, as you know it, progresses.

What is coming to you from me as you understand it is not personal. Josie has a great part in this action. Josie is sometimes slow to accept things that she knows inwardly to be true. She is weighing and balancing many things, or I should say, *all* things at this time, but she will win the battle more quickly than you can imagine.

Marie, whom you have been working with, is another who has a great potential. As a matter of fact, more people than you realize are close to this discovery. All souls have the Truth within them, but it is so far removed from their awareness that they do not believe it, or even know it exists. You are attracting those who are very, very close to the awakening stage. Just keep up the good work and do not allow yourself to become discouraged because you do not see evidence of greater fruitage.

I would say to all the peoples of the earth: "Be not too quick to accept those things which glitter or claim to be the *great secrets.*" This is the curtain that prevents souls from realizing the One Truth. Truth is not a secret, nor does it become gaudy and make claims of aiding you into the kingdom of heaven. Religion has made such a claim, and it only becomes a stumbling block to prevent the souls from discovering what it is they all have within them, but their eyes become so dim from the glitter of the world, that they are blinded to the real Truth. Even you, Wallace, can be quickly overcome by the temptation to do something or be something that you feel is worthy or great. Be not fooled by such clamor. The Kingdom, as the Master stated, comes forth like yeast and leavens slowly. Quick profits and quick gains are not the road to the royal richness of life.

Be extremely cautious of your temptations and desires to become great. You have learned many lessons along these lines, and I know that you have learned your lessons well. Therefore, do not be too critical toward those who, unlike yourself, have not come to this discovery. They will, in time, but not through your condemnation nor dislike, but only through your understanding and love.

One of the great lessons I have learned is that it was not meant for us to be so close on the human plane. We were close enough that we made the contact and a bond that was to become infinitely greater than any human friendship we may have known. Had we all been closer through the years, we may not have been able to make the contact we are now making. There was just enough closeness that a bond existed that will remain with no sorrow at any human loss. This is one of the problems people who wish to cling to the past are having. They feel all will be lost. They do not wish to depart from their old haunts and loved ones. Even though the bond between them was merely surface, they truly believed it was something more than that. I once thought I knew what closeness was, but now I see and understand that what I was seeking I actually prevented from happening; and that is what made me so lonely. Reach for the heights and never be afraid to part from that which cannot be put asunder.

April 16, 1984 / 4:25 p.m.

Hi! This is Katy,

All thought systems converge when not depending on the intellectual or rational mind. The human mind, as you term it, is merely a collection of thoughts, experiences, theories and concepts, individually conceived, which you term reason or knowledge. Such are not of the absolute, and far removed from such. It has been believed and accepted by human beings that each individual is separate and has an independent mind. This concept has prevented all thought systems from converging.

In seeking to explain the manner in which we, of this so-called side of life, function, you must realize we are of an entirely different nature. We are independent of the sense apparatus, therefore, we are free of temptations, vices and illusions as you know them.

Earthlings cannot comprehend how it is possible to exist and operate without a body or human mind. Just remember, we have no such form or mind with which to operate. You may wonder how such could be at the same time we establish conversation with you. Stop for a moment and ponder if you are hearing a voice speak to you? Can you see me with your eyes, or behold me with your sense faculties? You have your equipment, the five senses, all functioning, yet can you say you are at all conscious of using these faculties in which to be aware of my presence or my messages? I am coming to you but my presentation is not to your mind, as you call it.

April 16, 1984 / 11:00 p.m.

Hi! This is Katy,

Do not be deceived by thinking or believing that we do not have a body. Oh yes, we do, but such is not known by your intellectual line of reasoning. Just where do you think these messages are coming from? I am communing with you, am I not? I can feel and experience your presence, even be by your side and know your thoughts. Those who knew me when I was on your earth plane, believe that I am dead and have a body lying around, entombed in the earth.

I wish to remind you, that I am not the person you saw, talked to and knew at one time. I am still me, yes, and I still have a body that performs just perfectly. All the people of the earth plane have difficulty in understanding the true function and purpose of the body, for they believe that the physical form is real. In a sense they are correct, but their perception of me as I was, and still am, has not really changed. All that has been discarded is a human image of me that was incorrect.

Living on this plane, I have discovered the True Person is not limited by sense factors which completely distort the Real Image and only portray a false picture. You will be hearing more about illusions in the near future. I am being alerted to the false images human beings are holding in mind about the body. We have an opportunity here, not all of us . . . only those whose inner Eyes have grasped the real truth about the immortality of woman and man, that had its beginning where there is no time or space — therefore, is immortal and eternal.

When the human mind has been freed of all error images, beliefs, desires and impressions, that which is the Real Body begins to awaken and appear in all of its perfection. Herein is the work that is to be done for all residents on the earth plane, that they will come into their real body and no longer be under bondage to suffering, lack, sin, sickness and death.

All of us, yes, even those where I am temporarily residing, must go through this *transformation* in order to fully comprehend the meaning of all life and attain their divine Self.

April 23, 1984 / 3:00 p.m.

Hi! This is Katy,

I wish to alert you, at this time, of the impossibility of making the immutable mutable. This is consistent with all matter, time and law. You evidence the changeability of all matter. In your reference to time, you consider it as an ever moving thing. On the human level you also encounter laws that are being established, changed or altered constantly.

Human beings, since they began, have ever been in search of answers to the many riddles of life. Life is never really observed for what it is on the human plane. Individuals search out Life's existence and reality, but are unequipped to understand It's true nature. As a matter of fact, everything the human being seeks to understand is prevented, because it is *not* in his power to comprehend the incomprehensible.

These insights that are being revealed to you cannot be understood by the human mind. Because such matters are not understandable to the human mind, one must go outside the mind into the unknown to be able to glean any sense of rhyme or reason to what is being explained.

Mortality is a myth. To try to explain this to people is almost an impossibility. To try to state to you that you do not exist is not only unreasonable but pure nonsense. This is why the religions of the world have so much difficulty in trying to comprehend the measure of what it is they seek or teach. Such terms as "God" are wholly undefinable, and what is defined is certainly not the Truth nor close to the Truth.

You and many others are trying to understand how it is possible to exist without a body. The closest you can come is some imaginary being, but such is not clear. I, too, once wondered about it all, and with what little knowledge I have now about such matters, I find no way of trying to explain to you so that you can understand what it is I am trying to explain.

There does seem to be this veil which separates us. At least it does appear to you that way. From this side we have no difficulty. It just all seems so natural.

May 1, 1984 / 10:48 a.m.

Hi! This is Katy,

Reflect carefully upon the subject of our conversation of April 16, 1984. Due to the interruption, my message was not completed.

Explore the virgin territory of the subject at hand. You are wondering how it is possible to receive messages without the use of the human mind. First, let me say that the human mind is a collector of data, experiences, facts, as you would put it. Such is not in the category of wisdom or enlightenment. There are many areas in human life where ideas come to an individual without much preparation of thought or ingenuity in scraping together some formula or map. This includes such subjects as art, music, science, math, not to mention the various educational material that helps to enhance the earth's atmosphere. This is supposedly information that comes out of an individual's mind. It is, or should be, recognized as highly improbable for such wisdom to migrate or proceed forth from a mind that is merely a collector of memory of things incidental. I say incidental, as it appears very important, proper and factual on the human level. Such it is, I must state. But herein is the catch.

Suppose you remember you were given a Truth one evening, before you retired, that stated: "They are seduced by the intricacies of alternates." As you ponder this, you will see wherein what I am saying is true. Ponder this Truth carefully, and you will be able to extract the meaning of where ideas come from — not where you believe they originate.

Seduction is a matter of betrayal. One is very easily seduced, or led astray, by such things as inferences or influences that pass continually or rapidly through the human thought stratum. This is indeed perplexing, as it creates a confusion that alters the correct way of observation and the discovery of what is truly reality. The fact of alternates originates due to the mixture or switch of thought fields. There is really only one original thought strata, or mental ideas, that do not come forth from what humans consider *grey matter*. It would be better to say that ideas of creative nature come *to* this grey matter, but due to the subterfuge or interference created by the memory patterns of the mind, there is produced a rotation which causes a glandular distortion.

When something as intricate, invisible, invulnerable, as is an idea which presents itself to the human mind, which is, in turn, vulnerable and glandular, there is formed a toxic mental condition that is quickly resisted by the ordinary human being. There are many who are able to receive pure ideas and not place any foreign thought to them and thus produce some profound, usable material. This can be accomplished by you or anyone who is able to transcend the normal manner of trying to apply the *grey matter* as a proper receptacle for such celestial wisdom.

Put this in your own words, for what I am saying may not be imparted properly for you or other human beings to understand. (pause) For better words to explain my meaning, let us put it this way — it is extremely difficult for the corporeal to comprehend the incorporeal. Things invisible, so called, are usually a threat to the visible world. Human beings have difficulty in relating to those things which they cannot evidence with the sense mind. This is the difficulty with individuals who would like to understand this spiritual episode or revelation, but in translating the spiritual word they are unable to comprehend. Dealing with material forms is far more easy to understand.

Another way in which this may be more easily understood is the common expression used on earth . . . "You can't mix oil and water." Many try, and believe they can accomplish this task, but it merely ends in uselessness or empty wonder.

Only through transcending the ordinary method of using the human mind can this be accomplished. You may ask: "How does one transcend the human mind?" Herein is discovery and usage of a more rarefied structure which acts as a transformer so that the natural flow of ideas can come sailing in fluently and easily.

The suffering and pain human beings bear and endure is simply due to the limitations they place on themselves. Of course, they are not aware that they are causing these calamities. People in the entire world continue to run the old course and are afraid and hesitant to bypass or transcend these old methods. Whenever the human mind tries to project something, or anything, as far as what matters, they are treading on troubled waters. The human mind can neither project, invent, create, cause nor produce anything. That is simply not its purpose, but it proposes to be the source and desires to be autonomous. The world at large continues to build a trap for itself that it is unable to climb out of. There are a larger number of people in the world who can ascertain the more valuable and proper way of receiving the Truth which will set them free.

There is very little you can do for those who continue to keep on working in the old manner, enslaving themselves as they do so. Eventually, however, when an individual has hit the bottom and is willing to learn, the Truth is always there to reveal Itself.

The true heart and soul of every individual lies within the Truth of Being. All else is a lie and will never amount to anything but pain and misery. To accept this Reality is frightening, indeed, for the earth people. It means the loss of everything they have woven for themselves. Those still on the earth plane who have learned the lesson that nothing exists outside of the One Eternal Being, have a major and important role to play. It is more difficult for you to operate in this fashion than it is for me. I can relay this Truth to you with little or no difficulty. It is you and those on earth who have the responsibility of trying to open the way for Truth to be able to present itself individually. We here have what may be considered a difficulty, because we have so much to offer and share with the world, but only a few are willing, or presently able, to hear or understand what is being related.

This goes back to the subject of God. If only people realized that God is not some powerful Being or divine Entity that is sitting off in a cloud reserving all this Truth for selfish or personal glory. The world continues to entertain the belief that God is some kind of a Super Being with magic powers and keeps them stored up for only the so-called worthy or righteous. All Truth is available to every soul who ever lived, lives now or ever will live. God is neither a cloud, entity or separate being. God simply *is* and there are more people who are actually manifesting this Spiritual Force than you can imagine. The only problem is they are not aware that it is what you call God. They believe it is coming from their individual self.

Again, I wish to remind you that "They are seduced or led astray by the intricacies or entanglement of alternates which produces a rotating action." The divine in every human being can hardly be recognized or understood because of the clamoring grip of the glandular mind to distort each and every issue.

We shall meet again whenever you are in a good receptive attitude. Remember, I will always be present whenever you are ready to receive.

A grand display of non-attitudinal response.

K.

May 3, 1984 / 3:45 p.m.

Hi! This is Katy,

There are some interesting aspects you should be aware of. First, let me say, there are incidents going on in your ministry that you should be knowledgeable of and take the necessary steps to protect not only yourself, but the ministry as well. This is not meant to be alarming or something you should fear . . . only a precaution.

Not all of your students are aware of where you are coming from, and therefore, have difficulty in relating to your particular style of teaching. You have been made aware of this, and I just want you to know that from my place of abiding I can see all that is taking place. You have a way about you of presenting the exact Truths you teach to strike right at the core of the situation. This is good, but it might be well to soften the blows.

You must realize that you are functioning on a much higher level and what you say is true, but not everyone is able to comprehend the Truth of what you are saying. I am not even suggesting you change your style of deliverance. Truth is Truth, and not everyone is ready to receive the Truth. It is merely their own inadequacies that prevent them from taking a firm look at the situation.

It is well at this time that you minimize any contact with me in this respect. The Truths you deliver are O.K., but for the present moment it might be well for you, and others, that you not mention my identity. If there is any information that you feel would be extremely helpful, there is no harm in mentioning our communication. I am merely asking this for the general public at this particular time.

The odds are that there is beginning to formulate Itself on the earth plane, a new breakthrough in the matter of communication as we are exercising. A source of protection is needed to prevent you from being associated with foreign or false doctrines.

You will begin to experience a greater interest in the subjects we are discussing. Humans are slow at first to pick up on matters of this kind. Then you will discover those who grasp it quickly . . . sometimes too quickly, before they are ready for the experience.

Before the *after* there is calm and then comes the onslaught of the experience. You need not fear the *after* for it had its beginning in the *before*. It is always good to make your preparations in advance so that you will not need to go through any needless experiences that may be to your disliking.

Follow your inner guidance. Do not be too quick to form judgments, and above all, take time to sort out what is being revealed to you. There is no need for haste. You are dwelling in the time element, but, in reality, time is sometimes a stumbling block for the good Itself.

Friday, May 25, 1984 / 2:40 p.m.

Hi! This is Katy,

I want to converse with you on matters of extreme importance. I have been knocking at the door of your mind that I may communicate with you. Many interesting Truths are beginning to come to light and I want to share them with you.

It has now been one year, earth time, since I made my passage here. Like yourself, I have had time to reflect on my human life pattern, just as you are undergoing changes in your own viewpoint. You may find it difficult to rearrange your thinking pattern to conform to the Truths that are being sent to you and to the world, but just trust and be patient. You have been on the Truth path more than you realize, and it has taken you time to *trust* what is being revealed to you, because it is so foreign to your normal way of thinking and believing.

Josie is a nervous child and wants, more than anything else, internal peace. She need not fear. This is one of the lessons she has to learn at this time. She will endure her present suffering only to realize, as time passes, that this was her opportunity to gain deeper insight to those Truths which she felt she had already accomplished. Her one lesson is a deep inward tolerance so far as matters of love are concerned. She is a love child and has difficulty in realizing that not everyone else is so endowed. She cares and is more concerned than she realizes. Her interest lies deep, and it is difficult for her to understand how others can think as they do, not to mention their mental patterns and beliefs. This is all good. For, in a sense, she is absolutely right in being concerned, but not in the manner in which she is concerned. There is no reason anyone should allow themselves to have to endure the pain and suffering they are experiencing. Certainly they are learning lessons, but many times they do not actually profit by these learning experiences. They have to go over and over with the pain until they are willing to release the material sense of world and realize there is infinitely more to life than caring for the present existing life, which really isn't life at all.

The question asked by Marie is one of interest and concern. It is very difficult for the human mind to understand life without existing in a material body. First, I would like to say this thing you call a material body is not a body at all. It is a means of transportation given to each individual for gaining necessary insight into the full and complete configuration of eternalness.

You are beginning to come much closer to the realization that life is not really limited or confined to Matter, as you call it. The human mind does not have the equipment to comprehend life. It deals with only the physical forms, which are not real. You are absolutely right when you say that invisibility is the real and the Truth. This is quite opposite to what you see and know; you are not really seeing at all. If only you could open your eyes of Truth and really see what we all see here, you would be not only amazed but truly dazzled. This side of life is so absolutely opposite to what you know of as world. Nothing is solid here. There is no such thing as solid anything. This is a world of ethers. Nothing ages nor spoils nor decays on this side. Such things are unknown and are not real . . . only on your side of life do things have beginnings and endings.

I can actually be at your side and you would not be able to see me. Yes, I am invisible. This is not easy for anyone on the human plane to know or understand. You think of invisibility as nothing . . . no thing. How wrong this belief is. Invisibility is *everything*. It is *everywhere*, yet nowhere. There is no such thing as *nowhere* on this level. Everything exists at the same time and at the same place. There is no such thing as distance to travel or things to be accomplished or places to go. *Go where?* Here is *everything*.

The question I know you and others are asking: "What do you do all day, and do you sleep or eat?" Of course, that is a natural question for all earthlings to ask, as they spend their lives on earth encased in a form they call body, which needs things to do, places to go, things to eat, and places to sleep. Remember, we have no such form. Try to understand existing or living without some encasement in which to perform. It is much like the wave links operating on your receivers or radios on earth. All channels are operating at the same time, but they do not interfere. Each has its own position or wave in which to operate. They do not clash or conflict with each other, unless there is a disturbance in the atmosphere. We do not have such conflicts on this side. We do not bump into each other, yet we each exist and our energy frequencies allow us to by-pass each other or go through without any disturbance.

You can learn of this as you study the bird life on your planet. They operate by such things as radar or sonar. They can make their flight through the most difficult and hazardous environment in forests or the like, and can avoid objects or obstacles without any problem. They do not use judgments, decisions or compasses as humans do. They are equipped with the natural instinct to guide them on their course. There are times when they do wobble or get out of frequencies, and this produces accidents and collisions, but this is very rare.

The point, in thought here, is that everyone has a built-in energy frequency that can prevent them from meeting the calamities and trials of life that they find themselves faced with daily. The only problem is that they are not depending upon their in-born natural abilities, but are too busy trying to take matters in their own hands, which is one of the problems with intellect. Intellect can be very good but harmful if personalized or tampered with from human points of view.

Much more on this subject that I wish to convey to you, but for now I will release you with my blessings.

K.

June 14, 1984 / 2:30 p.m.

Hi! This is Katy,

What is so terribly wrong with life that causes people to have so much grief? There are countless conditions and situations that arise daily to cause people to fear and hate, not to mention the less responsiveness on the part of individuals, such as just plain old worry and concern.

Needless to say, I am aware of such happenings because, as you know, I was once faced with the same situation. That is to say, such responses are not exactly wrong, but are not necessary and merely impede one's progress, whatever direction they are going. This in no way is intended to create guilt or wrong doing on the part of individuals on the earth plane. Remember, the earth plane is merely a place of growth and development. Too many people make of it a place for pleasure only and do not take upon themselves the responsibility of crediting their lives with what is most important — growth and development of the individual soul. This is not intended to be criticism either — it is merely a caution to what causes needless problems that produce such negative and fearful reactions.

Now I do not intend to sound like an angelic prophetess or greatly enlightened spirit. In reality, there is no difference between me right now and the me that appeared on earth. The same is true of you and every other soul. That which has transpired in my experience is typical of all others. There are many, many things you, and everyone else, know, but have simply forgotten in the business of living the human life. If I were to tell you that this is not the True Way, you earthlings would think I was telling you a fairy tale. This message is being revealed on the earth plane and will continue to spread in a manner that will surprise you in the coming years.

I feel that you are looking for me to give you some *magic* knowledge or words that can help you and others. Rest assured, there are no magic formulas . . . no secret doctrines that can be of any real benefit to you. There is, however, within the innermost self of each of you, a storehouse and wealth of knowledge that can be of greatest help while on the earth plane. What I have discovered now is not really new to me or of any surprise. It was, however, seemingly veiled from my mind when I was encompassed in the earth atmosphere. It seems strange that I could not understand it while in human form. The psychology of human reasoning is coming close to the subject about what I speak, but there is infinitely more that needs to be revealed and disclosed.

All the people of the world are, more or less, full of questions which they already know in their innermost Self, if they will just take the time to reach inward and discover them. I have said before, there are no secrets that are kept from anyone. Everyone deserves the right to *know the Truth*. Too often the Truth is frightening to people, and they would just as well not even touch on the subject. The earth seems to have many more pleasurable trips and bounty to entertain them.

Take a moment and fear not to take a trip with me into what you call the unknown. At first, you or others may become apprehensive and decide not to journey into this territory. Stop for a moment and consider why one should fear this encounter with the unknown. Your first thought is that you will be deprived of all things known or familiar to you. It seems you are being invited into the never-never land where nothing exists. Wrong! Absolutely wrong! If the real truth is known, the people of the earth are living in the desert of time and aloneness. Many fancies and secret longings crop up to wet the human appetite and cause the individual to live in a proverbial land of make believe.

Why do you suppose people are so hesitant in meditating and pondering the true secrets and values of life? They honestly believe that only the earth plane has all there is to offer. To think of going into this nothingness or invisible space of meditation gets them nowhere. Those who endeavor to seek this path become discouraged, because they do not find what they are looking for. And what is it they are looking for but simply more of the fanciful things of the earth that so tatter and rust and are destroyed. Such a path is a blind one and leads to despondence.

Come . . . come with me into this seemingly empty void. There is nothing to fear. You will be surprised, once you enter this secret domain, what you will discover. I can assure you nothing you perceive here will be what you expect to encounter. Do not become sleepy, drowsy, and disinterested just because in your first attempt you do not discover what it is you are looking for. I can tell you this . . . what you are looking for is not there. The reason for this is due to the fact that what you are looking for does not exist and never did exist. Now, this can cause some to say that you would not find or discover or experience anything. I merely said that you will not find what you expected to find. This is the real culprit in the matter. This is where the things you believe to be true are not exactly true at all. They are merely illusions of grandeur. The things that are really good for people are the very things they shy away from. Strange, isn't it? At least that is what I once thought.

Now, just drift off into this, what you might call *nothingness*. Seems empty and dark in there, doesn't it? So at first you feel somewhat strange and out of place and a little disturbed and uncomfortable. Your mind will quickly come to your seeming rescue and present all sort of pictures and images . . . sometimes very weird ones just to entertain you and try to divert you from your real place of destination. Be patient; learn to quiet your thoughts. You are prone to watch your thoughts just as you would watch a movie — eager to see the next scene and to revel in your discoveries. Much of what you see is projected by what you *want to see* and not what is really there.

In your search in this *space,* do not try to see anything or try to do anything or try to attain or acquire anything. Just allow yourself time to acclimate yourself to this new environment. Surely, thoughts may try to intrude but do not give them your attention. As a matter of fact, you may even wonder what you are doing in here and what it is you are trying to find. Do not let this thought interfere with your seeking. Just be patient and willing to receive that which is seeking you. Yes . . . you are not in here to find anything as you might imagine. You are in here so that *something* that is seeking you will open out a way for you to be imbued with the Truth or knowledge that will allow your entire being to be revealed to you. This is not a matter of the search you think you are making. To enter this place in order to gain something or to find something or to discover some new truth is not correct, nor is it the object of your being here. You come here because *something* is calling you to enter. It has been calling you all through your life, and it is we who must open the door and admit what and who it is that is seeking to reveal itself.

Eventually, all imagery and thought will begin to subside. If they do not, you are not in a position to entertain the most important event in your life. If, at the moment, you are not making some kind of contact . . . do not be disturbed, and above all, do not force anything to come or to happen. It simply means that you are not, at this time, in readiness for what is to come. Wait until later when there is nothing pressing nor anything that may distract your attention.

Tuesday, October 30, 1984 / 1:00 p.m.

Hi! This is Katy,

I do not intend giving you a journal of my life experience but just wish to state that there are many incidents which give credit to the business of living for every individual.

It is good to greet you once again and to offer you any assistance possible on my part. I know you have been concerned at not hearing from me but circumstances made it impossible at this time. Do not believe that we are not still in constant communication. The bridge between your world and the world I am presently in is not separate as one may tend to believe.

The bridge between two worlds is a very interesting one. You are much aware of the transition that exists between the worlds. There are times when you tend to live more on this side than the one you are existing in at this time. This is not a criticism, as I, too, had experienced this when I was on your plane of existence. I still have many unanswered questions, and I have the ability to read your thoughts. I have never left you, and it is my good fortune to resume our communication.

To begin with today, let me explain the meaning of the trials and errors people seem to have to endure. I use the term "seem" because individuals honestly believe circumstances are thrust upon them as some measure of punishment or reward. Neither is truth. Every personal experience an individual goes through in life is actually self-inflicted. This is not easy for a person to accept, or properly understand, as it presents the idea that each one is responsible for his or her own thoughts. We all have a choice to make. This is true on our level just as it is on your level. Levels are, in one sense, no different as far as choices are concerned. There is infinitely more wrapped up in the consciousness of individual Being than even the most enlightened can comprehend.

Let me put it another way. You have often heard the statement: "There is nothing exterior to your being." Last Sunday you were discussing Existentialism. You were pressing upon the point at that time. Existence does precede Essence. I can honestly understand more of my true Existence now than ever before. What you term aura is but the essence of your Existence. Religion teaches that Essence is God and that it comes to an individual. True Existence means the Alpha and the Omega. The Beginning and End are really one, and nothing is divided. This has to do with what I was explaining when it was stated: *Exact time is a matter of sequential difference.* You and I, and all the souls in existence, had their beginning in God, in the beginning, which is past, present, and future. All that any individual is unfolding exists within them and had its beginning with God. Unfolding, according to earth time, seems to come spasmodically. This is only due to the ability of the individual to keep an open and clear mind for the revelations to come, unhampered. Earthlings are busy and preoccupied with business, trade, pleasure and many things to prevent them from allowing this perpetual unfolding to come ... not from some outside Power that seems to descend upon them, but a revealing of the Truth in one's *existence*.

Monday, February 11, 1985 / 10:35 a.m.

Hi! This is Katy,

It is more or less imperative that earth people should stand the responsibility of meeting any and all challenges that present themselves. This is of special interest to students who are developed spiritually enough. Those not yet developed will have difficulty in understanding the principles involved. This in no way is an excuse for not assuming the responsibility. Religion, as taught and described on earth, is relative to a God in heaven, who is responsible for answering the requests made by His children. This is not only dangerous but is untruth to say the least . . .

Death, as understood on the earth level, is far from complete, nor is it correct. On this side, we refer to crossing the time barrier. There is no such thing as death. If only earth people were aware of this Truth they would certainly eliminate a lot of sadness and despair. The subject of death is one of the confusing factors in human experience, and the religions of the world certainly have not enlightened individuals to the reality of the Soul's existence. There is no such thing as terminal. You hear much talk on earth about *terminal conditions;* as you will discover, not only in religions of the world, but also in the professional arena and among some of your material scientists. This does not mean that all those individuals, who are working in specific professional areas, are so indiscreet as to allow the common tenor of thought arrestment.

Enlightenment is the next step people of the earth must encounter. Right now, you and all the people of the earth are caught up in *thought arrestment*. This has become your culture. Much work is being done on our side to prevent such arbitrary refusal to clean up the mental atmosphere. *Thought arrestment* is so common among human beings, it becomes the *norm* to oppose any enlightenment filtering through. Popular, too, among peoples of the earth, is the establishment of certain cultures that out date them from previous bondage or enslavement to that of what they call freedom and advancement into the *new and improved*. There is nothing new. That which appears to be new is merely an improvement on that which already is. The Truth of that which *is* has been lost for eons, and now individuals are really trying to get back to the original plan of perfection.

A bird on the wing is going someplace. That does not mean a movement or transmigration from one region to another. It is merely moving through the passage way of existence. Herein has the term *time* been of a limiting factor. The time index, which earth people relate to in their every day lives, is similar to building fences and marking off different sections such as night and day, morning and evening. Time is irrelevant, but fits, very exclusively, in the duality of human thought. By this, I mean the arena of dualistic thinking, such as good and bad, right and wrong. In reality there is no good or bad, right or wrong. Such appears to be irrelevant to earth people, but has no place among the enlightened of all ages.

Time is an encroachment upon the flight of the bird. It creates parallelism, which not only hinders and restricts, but paralyzes the unfolding and becomes indexed in the *thought arrestment.* Yesterday is only a dream, an illusion if you wish to call it that. It happened but is an experience of the past. Memories of yesterday remain in an individual's mind to plague, tranquilize and decentralize the experience which each individual is to realize and experience. Tomorrow may be hampered by the *mental arrest* made because of memories of the past. Now is the only time there is, and it is an ever present experience. There are no walls or petitions; no barriers to hamper the bird in its flight.

From all of this you may glean the Truth that death is an impossibility. There is nothing that changes except the physical robe that is worn; the robe that you call a body. Physical appearance seems to go through a change, but it is merely a translation of what is for the ongoing experience. Just because you do not see, once again, your deceased loved one or friend is no reason to suspect or believe their experience has been terminated. Here is where we approach the subject of crossing the time barrier. The molecular or cellular composure of the human body is not reality. Herein is where you may refer to human and divine. The human is merely temporal power. Temporal power is not power. It is an arrestment in the time zone which creates the grand illusion.

You are receiving this because you are preparing yourself to cross the time barrier. This does not mean your exit from planetary movement, but rather your ascension from the bonds of time and space. Others, too, are beginning to receive this same message and are having difficulty in relating to its content. Yet, there is something within each of these which inwardly knows that this is the Truth, but due to *mental arrestment,* has a confused viewpoint in fully comprehending. It is similar to trying to remember a dream. Dreams are truly revelatory and have deep meaning, but when it comes time to apply the conscious reasoning to the experience, there is difficulty in translation. The true meaning becomes subdued and loses its component parts.

Time now for a pause. Remember, you are yet confined in the *time index* and it becomes tiring, even though the interest is keen, to remain alert to the messages that are coming. You will find that as you peruse this communication you will become more and more acclimated to the New Age Gospel.

August 6, 1985 / 12:15 p.m.

Hi! This is Katy,

Wallace, you are arriving at the place where you are able to discern some of the Truths that I have been unable to evaluate with you. I, too, have been wondering why our communications have stopped; and something in your consciousness brought this to light for me, and I know for yourself, as well.

We both have been working on the wrong track . . . yours of seeking to know of my whereabouts and the likes of what is transpiring on this plane. I was anxious to reveal to you the many experiences I have been having, and I, too, thought our communication was coming along perfectly.

What we are both discovering is the fact that there is no way to communicate real truth from one mind to another or from one dimension to another. This has been a similar, exploratory attempt by others throughout the earthly concept of time.

I was aware of a breach in our communication, and my attempts to break through were avoided both by you and me. I can imagine your concern about not hearing from me, and I was unable to do anything about it.

I should have realized from the beginning that my engaging in celestial matters was strictly not to be revealed in some bizarre way, but it was tempting and also interesting. You see, Wallace, the real Truth must come from within you, as it can only come through me. I have nothing to give you, and you have nothing to give me. What we are to know is already contained within us, and it is up to each of us, individually, to discern these truths. When we are on the same frequency, we can, once again, complete our work according to Divine Principle; there is no other way it can be accomplished. It is similar to like-mind, acquiescing and becoming one. Otherwise, there will be distortions and incorrect information that is relayed one to another.

I am not certain as to what wisdom you are tapping into, but I can rest assured that it is correct and encourage you to pursue this with all efforts to bridge the gap. I, too, am learning to do the same. Your vibrations are reaching me, and when this happens and I, too, can tune into the same frequency, there will be continued wisdom that flows. Otherwise, it is like trying to make oil and water merge together.

I had mentioned to you before that "there is nothing hidden that would not or could not be revealed." Perhaps now, when we have elevated our meditations, we will have less trouble. What is happening on your plane has nothing to do with what is happening on our plane. There is a higher dimension that we must work through without having any so-called knowing on our part. Knowledge is an interference with Wisdom. Wisdom springs forth from the First Principle and all else is inferior, if not untrue and unreal . . .

You can help me by helping your own spiritual unfolding, and the same goes with me. I can do nothing to you nor for you; and neither can you do something or anything for me. All each of us can do is work on our own awareness and unfolding, and then we will both be working as one.

Friday, July 18, 1986 / 1:40 p.m.

Hi! This is Katy,

More about Katy, as you once knew her. What you are about to discover has nothing to do with the demonstration of a person you once knew. What I am referring to is the continuation of the *life principle* which you believe is the body that now rests in the ground.

The Light that I am still shines in the darkness which you believe to be the one and only reality. The Light which I am is the same Light that you are. Encompassed in the framework of physical bodies and living in a material sense of world, is not the Light, but darkness instead. Of course, in your human perceptions, all look alive and filled with light . . . but such is not true. It is true to your view, but is not the Light. The Light is *you.* The coat of skin that you wear is hiding the Light that you *are.* No reasonable explanation has ever been given to you, or former generations, but the time is soon coming when a tremendous break-through will evidence itself. Many will believe, but still others will continue to believe it to be the work of fantasy.

The sun, moon, stars and planets all contain the same

radiant Energy and Life, but the reality of each is concealed. Exploration of their surfaces gives no reasonable explanation as to its true existence or originality. If it were only possible to reveal the many, many Truths available to us on this side to you who live in what we term *outer darkness* . . . it would be like a gigantic explosion to your imagination, senses and emotions. Emotions are not the same on this side. We still have feelings, but they are not suppressed as they are while living in a physical sense of body. Everything is made clear to those of us here, but is revealed in good time so as not to cause confusion. This is what is known by many of you as the sleep state that follows transition. It takes what you term a *period of time* for the soul to adjust or acclimate itself to this dimension.

As for form and shape . . . rest assured that each entity, soul, or whatever you choose to call it, retains and maintains certain dimensions. I can't even say it is comparable to the dimensions as you term them . . . but *It* is real and *True* and *Eternal.*

We can, and do, live among you as often as is necessary. This necessity is not for your pleasure necessarily, but for your development and unfolding. We can not do anything to heed nor stymie your progress, but seek to aid you if you are willing and responsive. It may seem to some that there is not much difference between this dimension and your dimension . . . that may be due to the fact that no amount of scrutiny or forbearance is devised. This may be easily explained in the way varying and different human beings view matters. Some have more appreciation for things celestial than others. There are those whose interest is terrestrial. This is due to the expanding consciousness of some, while others remain aloof to the great driving force of spiritual energy. In time, all will attain a greater atmospheric or spiritual climate and will stretch their now invisible wings and fly to the zenith. Wings but symbolize the effortless use of energy to attain what seems to be impossible. Clearer understanding and reasonable explanation will come when the soul is ready for expansion. It is much like trying to force a flower to grow or unfold its excellence and beauty. There are many factors involved here, as it is where you are. Herein is the governing Law of Expansion. Everything comes in its right time, and there is no use subscribing to any other methods. Patience is necessary, but a great amount of perseverance for Wisdom and Light puts one over the proverbial hump. Nothing is wasted, and nothing is undone, for the preserving principle of Life is the eternal grindstone, and molds all things into the correct stature.

It is not always easy to give up the consideration or belief that is uncovered. One has such a belief because it provides some payoff in the area of avoiding responsibility, blame, guilt, avoidance and fear of impact; or the debilitating self-pity of "If only . . . I would have been happy." The most devastating pay-off of all is the ego's insistence on its own importance, which is expressed as the attitude of *better than.* I have seen people who would rather die than to give up blaming a mother, father, husband or wife. And they died, unforgiving, for they could not forgive themselves. I am not saying that it is so, that sometimes people die rather than give up a belief.

You and I set up problems for ourselves to learn from. And each problem provides us the opportunity to become personally responsible for creating our *reality* exactly the way it is. If we refuse the experience of responsibility, the problem repeats itself later in time, often with different scenery, different characters, but the roles are the same. Only the names and the costumes change, and there is a compulsion to repeat our problem patterns.

When we finally look at a problem from the point of view of being the cause of it, instead of being the effect of it, we receive the gift of self-esteem and love.

We form our illusion-reality from our thoughts — those thoughts which become beliefs, assumptions, considerations, organizing principles, judgments, and evaluations. I will call beliefs all the kinds of thoughts which we use to structure our realities.

Where do our beliefs come from? They come from decisions we have made about how to survive. We not only make them up ourselves, but we are deluged with beliefs from our parents, from our families, from teachers, friends, books and society. Those which fit our unique decisions about making it in the world, we make our own.

Those which do not fit, we discard, make wrong, or disbelieve. Beliefs are not good or bad, right or wrong. They just are. There are beliefs which, when held to be so, limit our potential to expand, to grow, to experience the depths and breadth of our ability to love and be loved. There are other beliefs which are more fun to have and which we can use as tools, ladders, or stairways to expand and evolve. We cannot get rid of all of our beliefs. We can only take responsibility for them. When we do, the belief loses its command value over us as we shape our individual *illusion-realities*.

All of our negative beliefs and belief systems can be traced back to the fundamental notion that we cause nothing; that we are ourselves the result of our environments; that we have to dominate, sacrifice, put up with, or succumb to an essentially impersonal, unloving world.

This brings up a very nasty attribute of that part of us, the *ego,* for which pure surviving is the major issue. It goes like this:

"In order to survive, I must be separate from you; and I must maintain that separation, especially in a group of more than two persons. If I depend on you too much, or get too attached to you and lose separation, you could hurt me, destroy me, so I must, at all costs, maintain my separation from you."

Now what do you suppose the ego comes up with as the most efficient way to separate ourselves from almost everyone else? Think about it a moment.

It is this: "If I have an exclusive relationship with one person, that will automatically exclude me and maintain my separation from all others. And as soon as I have that exclusive relationship with one other, I have to start the process of separating from him or her to re-establish separation." Then comes the double bind: "I need you for my survival, and with you I may not survive. I cannot live with you and I cannot live without you."

September 2, 1986 / 10:30 a.m.

Hi! This is Katy,

Transportation is an important factor governing the world today. It becomes, therefore, necessary to reach out and absorb all the knowledge and know-how necessary to bring forth the best of two worlds. Those on the human plane are in need of better ways of living; ways that will enhance the ability to function in a more harmonious and orderly way. Order is necessary in the deliverance of overcoming the handicaps and obstacles that beset humankind.

The order of the day is transcending the ordinary method of growth and development into a more comprehensive study of the highest technique, skills and scientific innovative measures available. There is a procedure not as yet clear to the average human being. In this age of enlightenment it is being discovered that there is what I would call a "Transitional Bridge" existing between two dimensions. That is *this world* as the master called it and *my world* which is not of this kingdom. Just a few years ago, I, too, was a resident of the planet earth. Though not what you might call religious, I was especially fond of the *Lord's Prayer* given to earthlings from the Master Teacher, Jesus. In fact I was actually caught up in the necessity of repeating over many times this very prayer. It never occurred to me until shortly after my transition to this world, that I fully understood the true meaning of that prayer. A man that I thought highly of while a resident on earth, disappointed me sorely when he decided to delete the usage of that prayer in our worship services. It wasn't until I arrived on this side that I was able to understand how that prayer really affected me in a way that was later made clear. Now that I have a better knowledge of the meaning of that prayer, I would like to share it with you.

The contents of the *Lord's Prayer,* although it satisfied me dearly and brought solace, came to light when I was able to realize the importance of these few words: "Thy kingdom come, thy will be done on earth as it is in heaven." Now, mind you, I am not in what the average person calls heaven, but what I am observing far exceeds my concept of heaven as I once understood it. Heaven, to me while on earth, was merely an escape of human suffering and severity. At that time, I was in need of spiritual help and saying the *Lord's Prayer* seemed to meet my need.

I had been a firm believer in God all through my human life and the *Lord's Prayer* helped me to sustain that belief.

May 20, 1987 / 1:35 p.m.

Hi! This is Katy,

In response to the question asked you last evening concerning the disappearance of many people in the near future, I would like to respond. The following information I wish to share with you is not coming from my individual ability to foresee, but from the general atmosphere or mental tone that is being portrayed and experienced by the citizens of planet earth.

The answer may seem somewhat allegoric, but it becomes a true testimony of the culture and behavior of human beings who have strayed away from the true nature of their being.

The big exodus that is to take place, and the disappearance of their human instruments, does not necessarily refer to their displacement. Your question was presented as though they would no longer exist, and you wondered where they would be transported.

Their disappearance will be in style and not in nature. There is an increase in the disappearance of spiritual values in the planet earth. This necessitates a change that will enable all the citizens of earth to experience a growth that will enable them to realize the true nature of their existence.

This is not an act of God to be visited upon your people, but their own violation of the law of their divine nature. Many changes will inevitably happen, but it is due to the unlawful behavior of man. This is going to change rapidly, but not extremely, as you may well expect.

There is a movement of Divine Energy spraying the planet earth with spiritual dust that will act in such a way that there will be a transformation in the thinking and behavior of many. This transfusion-like spray will initiate a reform in the false beliefs and opinions of humans. Some will be broken by this inhalation of Spiritual Energy, and their vivid and false doctrines will begin to decline. Still others will quell their disobedient rumors, corrupt manners, and other devious thoughts and actions, and return to a more pristine conduct.

Such a mental change will be evidenced that you will merely experience a disappearance of fraud, hate, and adverse actions. In other words, those in high places who have been ruling the herd will begin to decrease. There will be a decline in evil actions, and thus the negative will gradually fade away. Do not forget . . . this will take what you on earth call time, but the die is cast and spiritual energy is coming to the rescue. In a way, this may seem like Armageddon, but it is a decline in the wayward actions of humans who have lost control of their spiritual forces.

Thursday, May 21, 1987

Hi! This is Katy,

There is a land of beginning again. A land wherein there exists a world complete of all desired dreams. The land of which I speak is not composed of rock and stone. It is not a world composed of matter but a world more real than one could ever hope for.

There are circumstances in life, to those who live in materialistic beliefs, that do not permit the mind to comprehend the depths or far reaches that one hopes to attain. Those who seek the spiritual path will be greatly pleased and fulfilled when they come into the understanding of the land for which I speak.

Circumstances are such on the planet earth that there must be a change of thinking and feeling in order to accomplish the desired good sought by all. Yes, every one on the human plane has a remembrance of the land for which I speak. They all ascended to it at one time and then, through some misjudgment or discrepancy, fell out of oneness with it and the realization that such does exist. Time, as you know it, has come for an awakening of the true realities of life. Many have become discouraged because their dreams of reality have not been fulfilled. Fear not, nor be discouraged, for approaching us is a revolution in behavior and enlightenment that will bring an end to all the heartaches and disappointments now experienced by those who truly seek.

Never, for one instant, allow yourselves to get into the mire of despondency to the extent that you become overly depressed. All of us on this side are much closer to you on the human plane than you may realize. The personal mind has difficulty in comprehending this fact.

There is a factor of emotions that must be understood in their right light. Emotions can be experienced on two levels of life. Herein is the confusing factor. We all have reactions and responses to emotions. Some are spiritual in nature, and others are attributed to the human or sense projections. To experience emotions is not to be denied as something that is strictly human. Yes, there are legions of human feelings, but there are equal amounts of spiritual emotions that act in more pleasant and enlightening ways.

For example, the human being is under the pressures of corporeal life and feels betrayed when not having his human desires fulfilled. This striving for excellence originates in the divine source. Whenever an individual is not experiencing this superior awareness, he feels naked and depleted. He feels betrayed, which is exactly the reason for not being properly fulfilled. Betrayal is due to the human nature's deportation from its original state of divinity. Humans are thus stripped from their divine equality.

One of the strongest forces within every soul is the need for love. Love is a natural and normal state that all should experience, and when they are not fulfilled, they retreat and become fearful and ostracized. This sets up negative vibrations that do not conform to their original divinity. There is a positive force field that carries its own polarity, but this polarity is not recognized by enlightened souls as something opposite or negative. Electricity, as known on the planet earth, has its positive and negative poles. The simple rotary is powered by this opposing nature, but it only applies to the material forms and not to the Spiritual. It is difficult for the human mind to conceive of this principle, because earthlings are accustomed to dealing in opposites, such as good and evil, up and down, black and white. These differences are looked upon as actual truth, which in reality is a misnomer. There are no opposites operating on the pure energy field. All is Light and there is no darkness. All is good and there is no evil. Such things as night and day do not exist on our dimension.

For example, on earth, people see the sun rise and set. When the sun arises, they call it day and when it sets, they term it night. The truth is, the sun is always shining, and it is actually illuminating everywhere, but is only experienced by those who are relating to form. There is what is known here as the *formless*. Earthlings do not comprehend such things or terms as *nothingness* or *formlessness*. Those who are composed of matter are incapable of understanding non-matter. The human is steeped in duality, opposites, good and evil. Not until a soul transcends the verbal usage of opposites will it be able to see true reality.

The same is true with the subject of life and death. Here we go into the same subject of opposites, which is known only to those composed or enclosed in matter. They look upon matter as one thing and non-matter as another. There is no such difference. There is only one true composition. The human mind cannot fully understand it, and, therefore, puts a label upon it.

As you know, I, too, once felt I was alive and was afraid of dying. Herein is a natural fear to all those donned in robes of materiality, or what you called "enclosed in a body." Yes, you are all enclosed in a body, and those on this and all other dimensions, likewise. The body you are now wearing is the only body you will ever wear, but it is not made of hands, but, as the Master said, "is eternal in the heavens."

You have been caught up in censoring this realization and have come a long way in seeking to understand its Truth. Keep up your efforts, Wallace. Perhaps you feel you are making headway in this discovery, and you must expect to meet opposition. Everything on the human plane has its opposites, which is the law of human consciousness. But remember, you and all others are only temporarily robed in human form. Your reality is never born and will never die. It forever remains the same, and in the experience of living and growing, eventually everyone will discover that there is but *one body* . . . and that is *pure energy*. The parenthesis, that takes place on the human plane, is only a dipping into the experience of living as an exile out of their original state of purity.

I, who speak to you, am embodied but not in the manner with which you are familiar. You think such questions as, "What does she look like?" "Does she sleep and eat?" and "What does she, and all those who have passed on, do all day?" Remember, we have no such things as day and night. Here we are, once again, into opposites, which is so difficult for the human to comprehend. I know now that I have the same body that I had while on earth, and which I had from the beginning, which is as you on earth understand. There is no beginning and no end. Another opposition. There is nothing but *continuation*. Changes, yes, but not extinction. Anything that is born will die. This everyone, in the human sense of life, experiences and believes. Not true.

So far as emotions go, many feel impelled to engage in the pendulum method. There is enjoyment in the opposition of the uppers and downers. Believe me, I once experienced this in my Cancerian nature. Riding the roller coaster of enjoying my sadness and my joys, my loves and my hates. Some are more prone to give vent to these emotions than others. We here are not on that escalation and de-escalation. Believe me, it is not boring here. We experience the stability in such a way that it is difficult to explain. Continuity is the normal. That is why those who discover the Higher Energies of Life are not concerned with laughter or sadness. They experience their True Self which has no awareness of opposites — only fulfillment. This is what every soul is seeking to attain, but they may become discouraged when told there are no opposites. Only through experiencing the *self* can one fully understand.

June 30, 1987 / 11:30 a.m.

Hi! This is Katy,

Most people on the human plane love to receive letters bearing good news. Sometimes information is revealed that has little interest or concern. I would desire to approach you from a symposium point of view. You, Wallace, have certain beliefs and ideas, and I, too, have feelings that may be of interest to you. I know you are concerned and tuned into my level of energy. Together we can share circumstances.

Many are confused about conditions on the level where I now dwell. Information that is revealed to earth consciousness usually concerns experiences from only one level of consciousness. I have found it so when conversing with you on this medium. There is infinitely more going on than what you have yet learned. The reason for this is due to the varying levels of consciousness on this plane. It is much the same on the human level. You may read in the print and hear on the news, about situations happening to others that do not relate to you personally, but only from a viewpoint of curiosity or news.

Up to now, I have only informed you concerning the

information being experienced according to my consciousness. Not all of us here are on the same level, or so-called environment, as you on earth would understand it. There are as many different interests and varying states of consciousness here as those on the human plane. This brings up a very interesting context, in which we may broaden our views and clarify much concern as to the going on from our dimension.

We experience here much the same as individuals do on the human dimension. Each is attracted to events and climate, as you say, so naturally they are only aware at first of conditions that relate to their particular level of comprehension and understanding. We have an opportunity to study, as you say, and learn whatever interests us. Some here, I have discovered, have no more interest in spiritual growth than they did on earth. Some have difficulty in adjusting to this plane because of their extreme interest in material forms as they once knew them. Oh yes, we have as much and more here than you do on earth. Do not think we are all living in some empty void with nothing to do. Everyone here is busy with his own thing. However, we are having to learn how to function without the human sense of body and without all the various forms of matter that we had on earth.

There is a limit to what we can do and experience here, but this is not due to any restrictions or limits placed on us. We are, in a sense, as limited here as we would be on earth, but it is because we have not yet learned to expand our consciousness. Having broken through the old beliefs, theories and customs, we can soar to any height with ease, comfort and security. We have an opportunity here to study, learn various skills and trades, medicine, science, building and constructing structures that we can, if we choose, to bring back to the earth plane for the building up of the human race. Here again, we have the choice. It is recommended that we engage in creative measures that relate to the successful survival on any earth dimension we may select. There are those who do not have to return to the earth dimension, in what is referred to as reincarnation, if they do not choose to do so. If they refuse to engage in mental or spiritual development, they only suffocate themselves in their own ignorance, and by the law of the universe, must return to other earth levels until they have learned certain lessons necessary to their own self.

You must understand the rule of existing on this plane is not necessary as it is experienced on earth. There is no cruelty here, because there is nothing of matter that is threatening or foreboding. The only main problem many have is the loss of identity with form and body. If one who arrives here is of an ill mind, they continue to struggle with the ideas and beliefs they have carried with them. There is nothing external to them. This is true on your dimensional level as well. There is absolutely nothing external to your being that has power, or is power, unless you elect it as such.

June 30, 1987 / 2:50 p.m.

Hi! This is Katy,

Before beginning any communication, such as being experienced at this time, I would like to share with you the composite requisite of this that I choose to call transposition. We are dealing here with a trans-communication that is new to you, and it would be well to explain the system by which this is operable.

There are many here who wish to communicate with loved ones or friends and find they can make absolutely no contact. It is the same situation I faced, when on the earth plane, when trying to call someone on the telephone and received no answer to my call. There is an interaction between two souls in order for a complete communication. There are many here who wish to contact someone on your plane without success. This is due to the fact that very, very few people on the planet earth believe that such is possible. Even when they do believe it is possible, there is either what you may term *static* or *skip* in the ethereal field through which energy waves transverse from one dimension to another. In order for you, or any others who so wish to make contact, there necessitates a completely free and opened mind to be a good receiver. It is far more difficult for you on your dimension to receive than for us here to transmit. We have little difficulty in getting our messages through. It is no fault or criticism on the part of those we are seeking to reach, other than that they are not listening or have their intent and purpose centered on other things.

You see, Wallace, we do not have those things on this dimension to contend with. Remember, I, too, lived the earth life, and little was I aware at that time of the possibility and extent of receiving words from those who had crossed the line. What I wish to say is that the listening attitude of mind is necessary for those on your level to be able to sense what great Truths are being spoken to them, but they do not have an ear or attitude to receive. The reason we are able to bridge this gap is because of your years of seeking beyond your world, and of your acceptance that "anything is possible to those who believe." You were quick to receive my message because of our vibrational attunement to each other. We, or at least I, was not as knowledgeable or sensitive to this fact when I lived on earth. It seems so easy now, and your receptivity to knowledge from the invisible plane enables you to pick up on me.

Try, to the best of your ability, to teach others the steps you have taken to bridge the gap between two worlds. I realize you are making this effort and have been so doing for years, but do not lose heart in your endeavors. There will be those who understand, and you must persevere with all earnestness in helping others to know that there is this region which is available for everyone to reach who have a mind to do so.

The correct method of communication, even on your level, is conducive to good reception. This should be brought out in your lessons on meditation. You already know the necessity of meditating on Spirit rather than on the things you want or wish to attain. All will be attained for those who steadfastly remain loyal to the One Self to the exclusion of all else. Remember, the Master said: "Seek and ye shall find." Our findings are not to be confined to the "things of the world" but rather to the "things of the Spirit." It is the Spirit of Truth within us all that we must seek to find and understand. There is no other place in the world to find Truth except in *yourself.*

Since being here, I have learned so much that I never realized before. I lived a somewhat secluded life and found pleasure in my aloneness, which at the time satisfied me, but there was the natural and human feeling of loneliness. How happy and glad I am for those sacred hours of being alone. It enabled me to get much of the human factor out of my consciousness, which enabled me to become more aware of the Presence of a much higher dimension.

June 30, 1987 / 7:30 p.m.

Hi! This is Katy,

Some supplementary material that I wish to relate to you is the disappearance of the body after transition. This, perhaps, is the biggest shock of all. An adjustment period of time, as you know time, is allowed to permit the soul to acclimate itself to the absence of a physical structure. In reality, there is no physical structure, but the mind, during its sojourn on earth, has implanted in it that the temporal body is real. I understand how confusing this is to those on the earth plane. The years they spend in tending and caring for the body establishes a belief that they have suddenly and somehow lost their human organism. Yes, it is just that, a human organism. Such does not exist on this plane, and when one has amply adjusted to these environs, it is not as distasteful as one may believe. The readjustment of the energy field allows the soul, through the resting period, to awaken to the realities that exist here.

Can you imagine the comfort and joy in not having to concern oneself about the physical organism and all it entails? No physical limitations to deal with and no fear of losing life or limb. Such things as food intake, concern about digestion or fevers, cold, cancers or threat of all the diseases known on earth are unknown here. The ethereal body, as you might say, has form, shape, and yes, dimension, but not so as is known according to earthly concepts and beliefs.

It has become clear to me that the earthen vessel, known as the human body, is just a shell and no more. All of its components, from bone, sinew, blood, tissues, organs, skin and so forth, are the by-products of the Life Force or Energy that comes from and is the essence and substance of Soul. Bodies, in human form, do not constitute life, nor do they furnish life. All life springs forth as the animating principle.

July 14, 1987 / 1:40 p.m.

Hi! This is Katy,

As I continue to learn and understand, the most important discovery in my life is to understand who and what I really am. This is not pertaining to me alone, but to every soul that has ever been conceived of God and by God. There are many interesting details to this discovery, and it is not yet revealed to many because of their disinterest in such matters.

The subject of space, time and form is little known by earthlings today. There are many, many theories, but none are correct. Science has yet to learn the intricacies of such energy fields that are unknown by minds that are subjugated by universe and man. Until this reality is cognizable, very little development will be disclosed to benefit mankind for ages to come.

Some progress is being made on the human level, but it is not sizeable enough to be recognized with any assurance or validity. The basic delay in the discovery by earth scientists is because of the theory of reality. The discovery of electricity was a revelatory unfolding; just consider how beneficial it has been to the earth sphere.

This is merely the beginning of greater energy forces that have absolutely nothing to do with the matter. The fundamental and basic substance of matter is totally unknown to earth scientists, because the premise upon which they work is merely a supposition that everything real is composed of matter in one form or another. Even electrical energy is viewed as some component of magnetic force. A magnet is composed of any piece of iron, steel that is induced by passing electrical current. Physicists work under the hypothesis that electricity is a property of the basic particles of all matter which consists of protons and electrons. Physics is a science which deals with the properties and interaction of matter and energy. Chemistry is also a science that deals with the properties of substances and their reactions, which produce or convert other substances. The placement or displacements of various chemicals or substances are calculated and labeled by specific chemical names. A number is given to the relative position of specific elements which is termed a table according to their weight and charges.

The world we as human beings live in, is certainly indebted to the discovery made by these major scientists and we are all benefitted by their findings which enables existence on this planet to be far more progressive, comfortable and practical. Without it we might still be living in caves, tents, or at least surviving in inadequate environs. So much for the positive progress science has set forth. A great concern of the earth people of today is posted as to the physical harm that is being created on this planet. The supreme Source of the helps and aids needed for earthlings does not have, as its primary source, a reshuffling of external measures but a complete change of attitude as to wherein the true restoration of power and authority originates.

If we engage in the religious aspect, as to the correct approach to changes, we will be in no better shape than we are now or have been for centuries. Scientific discoveries come closer to a solution, but their approach is hampered by their concept and belief in matter as power. There is a Power, and the wisdom to correctly utilize that Power to the advantage of all the peoples on the earth, that is currently left untouched. Neither science, religion, nor philosophy offers the solution to the redemption of all social, moral, financial, and other areas most stressful to humans.

POST-SCRIPT

This transmission began with the entity Katy, but it suddenly came to my attention that while the translation was going on, the energy projection of Katy was no longer present. This is the first time I became aware that I was left alone and the information being transmitted was coming from my own inner and Higher Self. I noticed the change, but failed to realize that the communication was not from Katy. Temporarily, I felt somewhat rejected. Meditating for a moment, I was informed that previous information was revealed through Katy, and that the time would come when I would begin opening the doors to the Higher Self within and would no longer have to depend upon the truths spoken by her or others. If, in case, certain truths were to come from Katy without my first being alerted or informed, her energy pattern would be presented.

Through these transmissions I have gleaned much information that was previously a matter of curiosity with no concrete evidence that such was true or even of my own imaginings. Herein is an important factor so far as to the reality of these messages; through study upon them, infinitely more than a theory or another belief has been revealed. There is absolutely no questioning in my mind as to the validity of what has been presented to me. I, in no way, am trying to influence you with these translations, or have any intention of persuading you of their Truths. My chief aim and concern is to present what you might consider a Philosophy of Truth that may be of assistance to you about the fact of Eternal Life. Naturally, there will be many who will discredit what they have read or are reading, but this is no concern of mine. I am positively aware that such is not for all people. Each individual in this world is on his or her own level of consciousness and will work out his or her own plan of salvation.

What this receiver has gleaned from all of this is the firm conviction that there is another Dimension yet to be discovered. The Master Jesus said, "In my Father's house are many mansions . . . if it were not so I would have told you." There are probably as many levels of consciousness on the invisible plane as there are on this dimensional earth plane. Is it humanly possible, of all the people on this earth, to find any two who are identical in their views, philosophy, politics, mannerisms, behavior or life-style? Naturally, every individual is hoping to find such for a mate, only to discover their differences, which seems to dispel what similarities they do have.

More important than any of this, is, to my discovery, everything in the Universe that we are aware of is material, right on down to the decimal point. It seems to plague us at times, make us happy at other times, discourage as well as uplift our spirits, only to end up in what we call death. Herein seems to be the dropping off place with no suitable explanation. The sorrow and grief follows when we lose someone we truly love. There are many such hours, days, months and years of feeling alone. To understand more clearly, know that another dimension comes into action immediately when a soul departs from its human vehicle. Yes, the human body is merely an instrument that we wear while traveling through this material dimension. It is given us that we may all learn specific and necessary lessons while on this particular sojourn. Never fear for one moment that the entity, soul, or one you loved has ceased to be. Yes, the human instrument is no more, and at present we do not have the faculty to discern the immaterial part which in Reality is the primary and principle part that is eternal. Those we love and who love us are not out of our attention. We may, through our concept of time, cease to remember them completely as once we did, but they are there along, beside and with us. They may live, to our knowledge, only in our memory, and we think the incident is complete. Not always.

Concerning the matter of those, whom to us, have made their transition, being close to us and beside us, I wish to make this statement: Although we cannot see or hear these individuals, they are close at hand.

Hi! This is Katy,

This is my Christmas Message to you and yours. So much thought and attention has been centered on the mystical belief in the Christmas Story and the birth of the infant Jesus. I use the words *mystical belief* in the widest of terms. Inferences have been made on the story, which, in its origin, was indeed mystical, but the world was not ready to understand the exact meaning of that term, which has grown extremely out of proportion into the modern day of commercialism. The *mystical incident* is still there, but the veneer of material thought has entirely covered the true meaning. The Christmas trimmings, Christmas carols and the wonder of it all still remain as it first happened, and the extreme extension produced by materialistic teaching has all but destroyed the natural experience. Such manger scenes are being discredited by many, which in a sense, is not entirely bad.

The New Age is upon us, and as I have mentioned to you before, "there is nothing concealed that will not be revealed." The earth is changing, as well as the consciousness of human beings. It was inevitable that a change would be wrought which seems rather devastating to many and pompously praised by others. The true believers need not feel discouraged or neglected. The real Truth about the original Christmas has never been properly or correctly defined. The reason being that such an event cannot be adequately explained to the human mind. The human mind cannot grasp the mystical teachings . . . that is, not until the mind is completely emptied of all foreign substances.

You were there . . . yes, you were there when it happened. You will doubt this, because, as I have said, the human mind, as you understand it now, was not there, and you have every evidence and proof that it could not have been. The event cannot be arrested in time. Remember, as it was said to you before, *Exact timing is a matter of sequential difference.* The *you* that was there is not the same *you* as you understand yourself to be at this time. Why do you suppose Christmas has been such a stirring event all these many years? The very event must naturally arouse many varying feelings and emotions. Each incarnation since that period quickens sadness, joy, wonderment, and misunderstood thought patterns. Some people want to be happy, joyous, sing, dance, and make merry while others feel isolated, alone and sad. The joy comes through an inner remembrance too deep to comprehend, yet a fleeting thought, here and there, too weak to recall in detail . . . yet it is there. The subconscious remembers when the soul of you was conceived in the womb of God. Sad feelings are the result of the time the soul departed and chose to wander on its own.

While the Christian world yet continues to celebrate the birth of the infant Jesus 2000 years ago, that is all they can remember of the event. They remain in total ignorance of their own birth as a child of God, which is meant to be the *Soul*. There is an inner tugging at the individual's heart strings to awaken to that very moment when the Christ was incarnated within them. Words cannot express the most thrilling experience of the birth of the soul. Perhaps music is the best way of recalling those precious moments. Oh yes, there was the music of the spheres — the like of which cannot be emulated. Many times, you, Wallace, have experienced those deep feelings when hearing certain music and cannot explain to yourself, or others, what is transpiring. There is very little difference between laughing and crying, sadness and joy. There is a polarization taking place. The thrill of being born a soul, and the sadness of leaving the habitation for more earthly experiences. This is happening to everyone. Many will not confess to such a reversal, because they have not awakened the learning centers within themselves. The New Age is going to be more revolutionary than anyone dreams.

Yes, Jesus *was* born that first Christmas Eve. This was merely the materialization of a Celestial Spirit. It was not the virginity of Mary and the immaculate conception of Jesus that was so spectacular as many believed. The star in the East, shepherds, wise men were not actually coming to witness the birth of an infant physical baby. They, too, were not enlightened enough to know what was taking place. They only knew something far greater than they had ever witnessed was being enacted. They responded readily to the inner prompting of something special, and it could be they knew exactly what it was — the celebration of the birth of every individual soul, but the writers of the Scriptures were not knowledgeable of the real miracle and stated that it was because Jesus was born.

Did not the Master say to Nicodemus, "Verily, verily, I say unto thee, Except a man be born again, he cannot see the kingdom of God." The birth the Master was speaking about was not the entry into a physical body . . . or some quick conversion as stated by others when they say "Born Again Christians" . . . It is the remembrance of that first and only birth of the soul that Jesus was referring to. To be truly reborn, as they say, is not the re-entering into another body or state of being . . . it is the recalling of the individual mind of that *first* experience of birth in the womb of God. To remember is to awaken to the realization of that jubilant happening — the Christian hymn, "Glory, glory, hallelujah! His truth is marching on." As the hymn begins, "Mine eyes have seen the glory of the coming of the Lord." And who is that Lord, but the soul of you? When our spiritual vision is quickened, we are not born, but are awakened to that time when we were one with the Infinite Presence. We are not only offsprings, but extensions of that very Presence. We are returning like lost chicks to the mother hen to be reunited, and remember when we were not separate from the Source, but conceived and developed in the very heart and soul of the Creator.

With this I will close and return to you again.

Friday, March 31, 1989 / 10:15 a.m.

Hi! This is Katy,

It is inevitable that communication should continue, even after this length of time, as you are accustomed to accepting. Adaptability is what human consciousness is undergoing, and it is well that the ability is to yield and accept what seems to be inevitable. Sequential difference, as we understand what you term time, is bringing forth to humankind a quantity of changes that were once squelched by limited understanding. With the speed of light these changes are being wrought because of the receptivity of Truth that is beginning to spread. Even your curiosity, Wallace, about life on the upper level is what enables you to more easily comprehend the tremendous quantity of ideas that are being exposed to not only your world, but the entire universe.

What you term the "Expansion Planet" is most correct and correlates to what Infinite Intelligence is seeking to reveal. Life on this dimension is so different from what the human mind perceives that it is difficult for the average mind to even comprehend. This goes back to your favorite subject, Anti-Matter. The earth itself seems to be a great mass of matter, but such is being discovered to be untrue. The human body appears to be part of this material matter, but the subject of what you term the "New Age" is alerting people to a far greater realization of what is actually true.

The brain of all human, animal, vegetable, yes, and even mineral life, is very much different from what has been accepted up to this time. All that exists has its beginning in a sea of Living Substance. That is about the only way I can even try to help you understand. Because the human mind is accustomed to dealing in mental diagnosis of matter, it complicates the correct definition or explanation of Substance, but that must suffice because of the barrier that exists in our correlation of subject-matter. You, like many others, are aspiring for more and greater understanding of this relation to material living and the transition to another as accepted and believed. Believe me, there is not the extreme distance or separation as commonly accepted by the human mind.

The human mind, as complicated as it has been believed, is but a prototype of the Astral apparatus, as you may think it is, to our ability to exist, experience, together with our ability to be and perform. It was once accepted that angels came and introduced themselves to humans, and these angels appeared to have human form with wings and were considered most unusual if not imaginary. We, here, do not consider ourselves as angels, but as Life-Forms that are quite the same as yours, but invisible to human sight and unknowable by minds that are accustomed to dealing with matter. The very interest in such a subject as we are discussing is ridiculous to many and quite insane and imaginary to others. Herein is the reason I express to you the inability of the human mind to understand or realize what is transpiring on our dimension.

The subject of channeling is quite controversial in

your world today, but the time is coming to you when you will get a much clearer picture and view of what I am seeking to explain. Do not confuse those who do channeling. There, of course, are those who are doing it for self-glory and misinterpret the entire meaning of what type of communication is transpiring. The very subject is interesting, and many are conscientiously attracted to this type of medium. Incorrect communication is not due to the ability to channel, but is produced by the receiver and not the sender. The gap between what you call heaven and earth is narrowing, and there is not the great gap between these two worlds as suspected.

Have you ever questioned where ideas come from? Yes, I know, Wallace, you have, but I am asking this question of the many who are beginning to realize more of reality. Ideas are particles, so to speak, of this Sea of Substance as mentioned above. They are comparable to fish in the sea, only we are speaking now of material concepts. These ideas are unlimited, and as humans receive these ideas and express them in application, they are merely bringing forth on earth that which exists in this realm. Can you now understand what Jesus meant when He stated, in what you call the *Lord's Prayer,* "Our Father, who art in heaven . . . Thy kingdom come, thy will be done on earth as it is in heaven."? Is not this channeling? We all have that ability when we make contact with the Power within and not the human mind, which is merely a receiver.

May 25, 1989

Hi! This is Katy,

The partition that seems to have been a separation between earth and heaven is being lowered. There is being exposed to the population of the planet earth, at this time, many revelations of Truth which have been heretofore limited. This, of course, is not due to the inability of Higher Energy Forces to reach human consciousness but the lethargy and indolence of human beings to recognize divine revelations. Due to superstition, ignorance and fear on the part of the human mind to become aware of spiritual factors, there seems to have been no communication between the two. This, however, has not always been the case, for there have been those spiritually enlightened throughout the ages who have been able to penetrate into the Divine. More and more higher Energy Forces are seeping through the barrier which the human mind has amassed because of outmoded and outworn concepts which have been preventing this illumination.

The New Age, that you of the planet earth are reading about, is just such a breakthrough and will escalate far more in your period of time. Religions of the older age are declining, because they did not pattern after celestial Truths but were regulated by the mandates set by organizations and institutions. Spirit has always been available, and all the benefits and rewards have and are existent to bring forth more peace, order, harmony and love to the planet earth.

Too many souls have been treading water, so to speak, and have been embroiled by social customs and mores and have drowned in their own ignorance rather than awakening to the Truth of Divine impartation. As your part of the country celebrates Memorial Day, seek to realize that such attempts have been made on the part of many who have given their human sense of life to protect their country and their own. The cry that has been heard over and over again, since the advent of man, is for *freedom*. How many have tried to understand just what freedom they are seeking? The entire world has been captivated by rhythmic movements of interplay regarding the human nature of being rather than the discovery of the Divinity of being.

In our inter-planetary communication, as earthlings speak of, is really an interplay of Inner Cosmic Connection. More and more you are seeking to uphold and defend the subject of the New Age and rightfully so . . . when it is clearly understood. New definitions of words, as well as new words themselves, are surfacing more and more. The reason for this, as you well know, is not truly new, but an expansion of man's understanding of reality.

The word Cosmic as defined in your dictionary, fails to define what is taking place, as it always has, on the higher dimension. This is due to man's misunderstanding of Spirit, or as you call it, Anti-Matter. The word Spirit, as once understood, is a misnomer due to the belief only in matter as reality. Reality on the human plane is just a degree lower than the upper level. You have been relating recently with polarization. These are not external differences, or a position that is diametrically opposed to each other, merely different degrees. Once again we are dealing with the time index. *Exact time is a matter of sequential difference.* At one time, it was thought insane to believe that it was possible to cross the United States in a matter of a few days. Flying was also considered impossible, not to mention the ability of man to reach the moon.

January 31, 1990 / 11:45 a.m.

Hi! This is Katy,

What is about to be disclosed at this time, may be perceived by the majority of human knowledge as a conspiracy against any or all who know philosophy, religion, science, yes, and even metaphysics, as it is being perceived at this advanced age.

The belief syndrome accepted and endorsed by any and all manner of human conception is, and will continue to be, a threat to humankind until the veil is lifted that reveals the Truth of Being. In your present social order, and this has reference to all traditions, customs, forms of worship and beliefs in God, there still remains invalid information as to the Source and Cause of all that is.

The very teachings of Jesus Christ have been misinterpreted and misunderstood all these centuries and will continue to be so until the barriers of Truth are made clear. Your human sense of time is edging closer to the Divine edicts and proclamations than at any time in modern history. At present, the planet earth is too absorbed in obtaining those things which will not bring happiness, peace and love. By planet earth, I am not referring to the earth itself, but the concepts held by humans who came *from* the earth, such as all forms of animal, vegetable, mineral forms. It is true that the earth is the footstool of God and remains at the base of all matter. Such things as atoms are all basic forms that can be transmuted into everything that human beings are searching for — but do not find. The earth is an organism that continues to house, feed and provide a dwelling place for those who are yet in the human dimension. The human body contains all the elements that are found in the earth. Out from the very dust of the earth there dwells the components of the material body. "Ashes to ashes and dust return to dust." This does not infer that ashes or dust are unholy or bad. It simply means that this is the very substance from which the body is formed. There is nothing immortal about human form. Herein lies the crux of understanding Reality.

Friday, December 28, 1990
12 Noon

Hi! This is Katy,

New Year, as celebrated on the earth plane by human beings, is a misnomer according to the Higher Dimension. To earthlings, it is a time for new beginnings. There is certainly nothing incorrect about expecting a better life in the future. The error lies in looking to a time element to bring forth greater blessings. Correction in old habits and old beliefs has nothing to do with time. The real solution lies in a complete change of thoughts, which has to do with shifting one's consciousness from the material dimension to the Higher Dimension. This is not easy for those who have little or no understanding about how the mind truly functions.

This brings us to the subject of change and the belief that *thoughts are things*. Thoughts are simply things which can add to the unfortunate outcome of any endeavor. The human plane is coming into the awareness of the powers of the mind and needs to realize that the mental plane is merely a step to the ultimate Spheric Truth.

On the place where I now exist there is no mention

of thoughts or anything concerning matter or material things. On arrival here, one soon learns that this plane is completely different from the earth plane. It is difficult to explain in detail just how those on this level successfully operate and function. The human mind is ignorant of our laws, because human interest is directed in matter in all of its forms and dimensions.

To be successful in the New Year, as humans present it, is not a matter of positive thinking, however that is far better than concern with the negative attitudes and beliefs.

Tuesday, February 12, 1991
12 Noon

Hi! This is Katy,

The lag in communication that has been existing for you on earth-time has been somewhat of a mystery to me as well as yourself. Although there are extreme differences between the earth plane and the plane wherein I presently exist . . . there are similar reasons that prevent an even flow of a reasonable dialogue. On the earth plane there is what is known as time-warp, which delays not only communication but the function of electrical, mechanical, and even biological relay of evenly distributed activities. Something similar exists even on this plane, which when clearly understood, is a resting period wherein spiritual, mental and emotional growth can rectify itself and produce a greater expansion and growth.

Such an experience is confusing to the human mind and all of its aggregation of thoughts, emotions, and belief syndromes. Such is a subject which I would like to share with you at this time.

The subject of faith, as I understood it on the human plane, was very important to me and somewhat puzzling as I matured. Without a much clearer understanding of the term faith, conflict can be produced in one's thinking and most traumatic to the human emotions. Faith is very essential and necessary to those in the beginning stages of their spiritual unfolding. Although extremely beneficial in one's earlier stages, and sometimes more important in advanced human analogy, it is a phase of growth in attaining enlightenment.

Religious terminology, on the human plane, emphasizes the importance of having faith in God without explaining more precisely who and what God constitutes. In seeking to understand the nature of God, to those who are novices in transcendental matters, there looms in the human mind a barrier that needs to be enlightened. To the mortal mind, experience is more valuable than wisdom. The Infinite is a Divine Wisdom that comes forth like "yeast that leavens," as Jesus mentioned. There is more concern, on the human dimension, to experience the vast array of human feelings and emotions that in one's early stages is devoid of wisdom. Herein is the problem confronting human beings.

Thursday, April 24, 1991
10:10 a.m.

Hi! This is Katy,

The narrated experiences explained and described in this work came about in a most unexpected way.

First of all, I would like to identify myself. I have been known to my husband as Katy. I am speaking now in the present tense, but I left this earth plane back in 1983. Little did I know at that time what wonders could possibly transpire after my transition. Let me digress in your sense of time for a spell.

Looking back at my human life experiences, they were no different from the average person who encountered many oppositions and challenges. The main concern with me was a congenital heart problem that restricted me more and more as I matured. I was diagnosed as having two holes in my heart. In my more secluded life, even though I was married, I became interested in music and art. There was an extremely lonely feeling I seemed to carry with me, and I found many helpful hours through my paintings and through my piano teaching of young people.

In my later years, I became interested in the metaphysical study and became a member of Unity in Toledo. I attended classes taught by Rev. Tooke and attended Sunday Services and even played the organ a number of times. This was my introduction in acquainting myself with what later would be my enlightenment. Before the great event took place in my life, I was often irritable, quick tempered, and judgmental. Through all of this, a period in my last few years on earth brought to me a realization that there was something more in store for me than just living a normal human life. There wasn't much in the human world for me to enjoy because of my physical condition.

The reason for informing you of this is due to the fact of what transpired following my transition. Prior to this time, I became interested in the Truth teachings that I had acquired in my association and affiliation with Unity as taught in Toledo and reading the periodicals from Unity School of Christianity, located in Unity Village in Lee's Summit, Missouri.

My husband and I had been close friends of Wallace and his wife, Josie, for several years. Little did I know the love Wallace and Josie had for me and my encounter with the Truth; and that they were seeking not only to teach it, but live it as well.

The reason for my disclosing this information is to explain just how the narrations in this book came forth into expression. I can assure you that neither Wallace nor I had any intention of revealing these discourses. Wallace was reluctant to reveal what transpired except to his wife. As time passed, Wallace became more interested in what was being revealed to him and was reluctant, at first, to completely believe all that had taken place. I will close my comments at this time and let Rev. Tooke explain just what has transpired.

April 24th, 1991

It all began back in 1983. For some time my wife, Josie, and I knew that Katy was having severe physical problems with her heart. It became obvious to both of us that she was, unconsciously, informing us that her life on earth was near an end.

Shortly before her transition, Katy was in the hospital several times, but she was never incapacitated. She had a strong will and was determined to live. Despite her intent to survive, my wife and I detected a behavior in Katy that indicated she was making preparation for making her exit. During that time I went over to see her; she was then having difficulties, and I asked her if she was afraid or had thoughts of leaving this world. Katy said, "Oh, no, I want to live longer." I immediately dropped the subject, and we talked about other things. One week before the final day, my wife invited Katy, who was alone at the time, to come over and have dinner with us. She gladly and willingly came — not knowing that this would be our last encounter with her, and she with us.

W.T.

July 21, 1992 / 3:00 p.m.

The transcriptions enclosed are from one who has crossed the Transitional Bridge to help lessen the fear of those who are reluctant to make such a journey. For this reason, these messages are dedicated to those who remain on this side of the Bridge.

The planet earth may be compared to a gigantic airport that encircles the entire globe. Daily, hourly and moment to moment, there are departures and arrivals of souls that have come from some place or are going some place.

Meister Eckhart, a thirteenth century Dominican Catholic priest, says, "If a man's work is to live, it must come from the depths of him, not from alien sources outside of himself, but from within."

The transcriptions enclosed are for those who have not prepared an agenda for the business that lies ahead or even thought of acquiring an itinerary for such a voyage. All the peoples of the earth know what is told them by the clergy or fearsomely conjured up by their own imagination. The Master Christian talked about such a place, but the number is legion of those who fear that they will not reach such a place. Even if we reach heaven, as it has been described to us, it doesn't appear to be as appealing as living on this earth planet, despite the problems citizens of earth are experiencing. All the religious teachers of old, even with their surreptitious and sacred writings, fail to encourage the majority of earthlings to attain the desired good they are unanimously seeking — Nirvana. Instead, the fear of death, Satan, evil, yes, and even God, has fractured the minds of many. Xenophobia, which is fear of the unknown, has become the mind devil, God, and paralyzes every desire to know oneself and oneness with God.

The new order of business among quantum physicists is giving insight into the so-called unknown, which may very well usher in an era known by many prophets of old; the subject is mysticism.

W.T.

August 5, 1992

"I must give it to you in blind, by the Neptunal Sea.
A colorful array of pictures."

The message stated above came to me at first as a mystery; an explanation follows:

Three months following Katy's departure from this earthly plane, Will, her husband, mentioned to me that a container filled with Indian Head pennies that Katy had collected and was very interested in, could not be located. He searched the house and was unable to find it. Katy had shown this to Josie and me several years before her transformation, so I knew of her delight in this cache. Several days later came these words: "I must give it to you in blind, by the Neptunal Sea. A colorful array of pictures."

I had the feeling this pertained to the missing Indian Head pennies, but I was at a loss to interpret the message. My human reason began conjuring up all sorts of explanations . . . "You wouldn't hide pennies by a blind . . . and what did the Neptunal Sea have to do with it? What did the array of pictures mean?"

Several days later, Will told me he had found the cache

of pennies. I asked him where he found them. He said that he found them in the basement under a stairway of several steps. At the time, this did not register in my mind as an answer to the riddle: "I must give it to you in blind." Well, "in blind" had nothing to do with a window blind, but rather with being hidden. And then I realized that just a short distance away water pipes were coming out of the ground up through the basement floor. So that solved the explanation of ". . . by the Neptunal Sea," Neptune having to do with "Sea God." So that explained the water pipe. Will said that the pennies were behind a stack of unframed paintings that Katy had painted. So this explained the "colorful array of pictures."

This was my second verification from Will that the transcriptions were not my imagination but something of an entirely different nature. Although I was deeply moved by the messages that were coming and the awareness that this was far, far more than I had ever previously encountered, my mind was in a quandary and thoughts of doubt about all this tried to overpower me. But as time passed and the messages kept coming, my faith and confidence grew with leaps and bounds. I knew this was a passageway enroute to what I would like to call "The Transitional Bridge." Herein is one of the reasons these transcriptions had to be released to all those whose minds and hearts are open to something of a link between two worlds. At first, I had made up my mind that these messages were for me alone . . . that is, until I realized that, although they may have been intended for me, they were for others to hear and understand as well.

It wasn't until the fourth transcription came on August 3, 1983 that the words, "Hi! This is Katy" preceded the message. From that time on they all began with "Hi! This is Katy," and it was explained to me that to insure divine protection I was to hear these words of identification.

This will explain why the message dated July 12, 1983 came as it did — questioning in Katy's message as to why she was unable to reach Josie and me at that time. When she said, "There is a guide which seems to be informing me of certain transgressions on my part. Help me to understand this mystery; something I must have done or said complicated this blockage. Help me, please." Being a new arrival in her higher dimension she was not at this early stage knowledgeable of certain "rules" she was to follow. In any event, the correction was made and this was perhaps because she needed to identify herself.

This gave rise within me as to the many unknowable knowledge principles to be obeyed on a higher dimension. More reason to believe these messages were of divine origin, or at least permissible.

W.T.

Hi! This is Katy,

Your earth-time has lapsed as far as our communications are concerned. You need not be concerned when I say that for now this is a farewell message. Our work together, by your present sense of timing, has been completed. You have only to remember that *Exact timing is a matter of sequential difference.*

For now . . . you have been a recipient for the necessary information that is to be distributed to the peoples of the earth-plane. This, however, does not mean that there will not be a continuing biographical communication whenever there is a need.

You have followed your instructions well and have faithfully set forth to perform exactly what you were chosen to do. You see, Wallace, neither you nor I have taken it into our personal self to relate these transmissions. There is infinitely more to be revealed to humankind, and it will be forthcoming when the consciousness of humans is ready to receive the Truth.

The Overseer, if you may call it that, has always been

willing to reveal all Divine Revelations when students are open and ready to receive these Truths. There are many on your earth plane who shun the word God or anything that refers to the Infinite Cosmos. The many changes that are taking place on the planet earth are preparatory steps necessary to bring enlightenment and to awaken Souls to the real Truth of Being. Whatever name you give to the Creator is unimportant. That is to say . . . God has no name. God is nameless. Names are given to personalities whose only way of identity is through the use of names. All the religions of the earth have this particular name for the Infinite and so they become vernacular — prejudice and fear grow from searching for the meaningless, but still we cling to specific names. Just as you call me "Katy" and I call you "Wallace" is merely for identification of the human personality. Having crossed the Transitional Bridge there will always remain *identity,* but not in the manner to which you are accustomed. There is but *One Infinite God . . . One Infinite Soul,* and *One Infinite Body.* This is difficult for people to understand, and it is up to you to seek methods and ways of disclosing your identities.

No one ever completely loses their identity. The Soul of everyone is that which is made in the image and likeness of God. It must be made clear that God did not make a body. It is not the body that is made in the image and after the likeness of God . . . *It is the Soul.* The Soul is ever one with God which *is the only begotten.* I have made mention to you of this matter when I said you would not know me as I am. I am the same as I have always been, but when a Soul comes into the earth atmosphere, he or she has put on a cloak that is called a body and is known by his or her name, shape, size or color. Such is not the case. The body on the earth plane is a visible manifestation that depicts and exemplifies the growth and unfolding each individual has accomplished on the rung of the ladder of life. The Spirit, Soul and body each formulate the unity of the whole person and should never be separated. The awakening will come when we no longer need to shed the outer structure we call the body. This, however, will not be completely accomplished until we, like Jesus, have overcome the world. That is to say, rising above every human error and discord, and ascending to our rightful identity as the only Begotten Son of God.

K.

Afterward

Thanks, Katy. This is Wallace. This has been quite a journey. There is a Transitional Bridge that exists between two worlds. One is the material sense of world in which we humanly dwell and the other is the world of non-matter. Up to the present time there has been very little said about an anti-matter world. There have been names given to such an imagined world, such as *The Kingdom of Heaven, The Other Side,* and others to label a supposed existence beyond this present one. Physicists and scientists do not agree that there is such a dimension, but that is no reason to diminish the idea that such exists.

There are different theories concerning the existence of non-matter or anti-matter, but currently there is no evidence or proof. Most professors of all the major universities cannot accept this anti-world as there is no way of proving that such exists. Discussions have been made concerning the "Big Bang Theory," but it is too early to calculate their hypothesis. Some scientists declare that matter and anti-matter cannot exist in the same place at the same time. Others give it the name of "Shadow Matter." The average human being is left with doubt and skepticism as to such a world, and that is easily understood. After all, every human being is composed of carbon based substance such as our bodies, the world in which we live, and things of which the world is composed. Whether it be mountains, streams, deserts, plains, or oceans, each and every one can be analyzed and given some atomic substance or chemical identity. The theory at present is that everything in the universe is composed of matter. We must not become disposed to give up the search for Reality and depend on intellectual minds to reveal the Truth of all being. Now that doesn't mean that all intellectuals or scientists are without question or beyond the ability to understand infinitely more.

Scientists and physicists are a special kind of people. Those dedicated to the discovery of the elemental structure of this material world, biologists, chemists, physiologists, psychiatrists, metaphysicians, are all in search of the substratum element of the corporeal world. After all, it is in this dimension where we all reside at this present time. There is need to understand our basic human element, for without it mankind would be really floundering. The major questions come to those who, at some stage begin to question, "Is this all there is?" "Then, what?" Religion and philosophy have their fingers in the pie as well. They are seeking for survival not only in this world, but also in the world to come. They offer comfort and solace to those who are traumatized by their existence in this world and hopefully, wish to attain a better world that they can call the "Kingdom of Heaven." Are we not all in this dilemma together — saint, sinner, philosopher, scientists, working men and women, even our offspring?

I, too, am a journeyman on this pathway of life, but the question has arisen in my mind as to the distinction between *Life* and *Living*. Back to the platform on which we all stand between two worlds. Is there a dimension that exists other than this material world? What is the relationship between past generations and present ones? Where is the past and those we loved who departed from this world? Is it possible that another world exists? If not, what is the elemental form of the material world, or whatever you choose to call it? We all exist on terra firma, but where are the races that existed here? What of their culture, politics, monumental structures, social, economical and industrial civilization? Is all of this extinct, or is it a matter of modification and advancement?

We hear talk from other arenas that there is no such thing as time or space; such could be a matter of abstraction. There is no past or future. Everything and everyone exists in the eternal *now*. We are probing some mighty steep areas here, but is not this our right as citizens of Earth? In a sense we are all miniature scientists who are seeking answers individually.

The search for the meaning of life has been going on for ages, and continues to do so, which is our prerogative, and will possibly go on throughout infinity. We can refer back to the Sanskrit, ancient teachings of the Hermetic lore, ancient Egypt, even the Greek philosophers. Saints and seers of every denomination and religion play a part in the search for the riddle of life. Is it now time, if we can refer to such a dimension, that mankind is awakening out of some lethargic state, to a much higher dimension? We have evidenced the past few years, the tremendous advancements made in upgrading this world. It is as though we were entering a time warp that accelerates us into the field of energy that is not composed of matter. We can be assured that there is energy that is not derived from coal, oil, or any other material substance.

The element of Life is not made of the same consistency as the element of Matter. Life itself cannot be analyzed nor probed, because we are speaking here of that which is not composed of chromosomes, protozoans or some cellular structure. Life is really an invisible source or energy that must be considered anti-matter. There is no physiological form that may be observed, x-rayed or dissembled. Things living are but manifestations in varying forms and degrees of an element called Life. Living things are alive so long as the element Life is present.

The moment the properties of Life remove themselves, the living element engages in the cessation of vital forces.

Examining objects, worlds, civilizations, people, friends, loved ones past, there is no visible or tangible evidence of their existence. Only a memory of them, like a dream, remains.

As this material has been assembled, it has been as though thoughts, impressions, and information are being revealed from some concealed Source. Mechanically speaking, we all know something about how this world ticks, but we move about like zombies without any awareness of how or why. It is obvious that our ignorance of the vicissitudes of life are causations of some force of which the world of matter is totally unaware. How is it feasible or possible to define, describe or analyze something that is totally non-existent? One has to see it, hear it, or touch it, in order to probe its content. It is possible to dissect the human organism and its vital parts, and to detect symptoms or causes of infectious germs or deterioration. This includes such organs as heart, lungs, liver, kidneys, stomach, blood, bones, skin and hair. But are we not referring to some corporeal substance that is the unseen nucleus of material bodies being those of not only humans, but animals as well? How is it possible to even conceive of examining such as an anti-biophysical substance? It is like trying to define or describe nothing. Nothing is nothing. Yet there is something unknown to human knowledge.

Life cannot be defined properly, because there is no known instrument capable of observing it. Such is true with love. Poets write about it, preachers promote it, people pray for it, many think they can define it, but how can you describe or explain something as intangible as a non-particle element? Humans prefer to speak of love as a matter of persons, places or things, all of which is composed of matter. Love is indescribable, yet we continue its search and will continue to do so.

Wisdom is also an invisible quality. You can gain so-called wisdom by reading books, going to college, studying, etc., but eventually you gain an experience of an invisible something which we term wisdom. No one has seen wisdom, yet we all claim to have it or know of some individual who is wise, learned, or excels all others. Are we not speaking of a human being with a collection of fact? The human form has a collection of wisdom, but that is something invisible that is registered on the brain-cells to come forth later with greater knowledge.

Much of what is being stated here is a culmination of questioning, searching for answers outside of the realm of reasonable matter-stuff. A break-through in the great energy field is emerging. Mankind is standing on the brink, a transitional bridge between two worlds, and what is about to be discovered will revolutionize the world. The illumination that is being released has come to this time to bring the world out of the doldrums of indolence, superstition, fear and ignorance and awakening to a whole new world of infinite possibilities the like of which we have never dreamed.

My search had led me to the brink of self discovery, but a chasm appeared too deep and vast for me to penetrate until the experience which this book relates. The matter-self of me, with its mind and body, stood on that transitional bridge between two worlds, but it took something which I term a non-material being to enlighten me and to share with you. It is difficult, is it not, to imagine a human being you once knew or loved to be any different from what they were. We can or could imagine them in heaven flying around with wings, which also involved matter-form. It is difficult to erase from human consciousness old patterns and beliefs which we have sheltered throughout the years. We may realize that they are dead or that their body is resting peacefully in the grave while we continue to visualize them as we once saw them — but from here out there is a blank.